"I always enjoy reading what Jennifer Kennedy Dean writes because it is always biblically accurate, deeply profound, and invariably inspiring. She has done it again in *Altar'd*. This book is filled with nuggets that will inform and change your life. I highly recommend it!"

—*Dr. Richard Blackaby, coauthor of* Experiencing God, Revised Edition, *and* Spiritual Leadership

"Jennifer Kennedy Dean has written a powerful 40-day devotional book which is one of the clearest teachings on the difference between the flesh and the spirit I have ever read. You will be forever altar'd after reading this book."

—*Carole Lewis, First Place 4 Health national director*

"Forty days of WOW! I can count the number of books I'd like to read twice on one hand. Yet I can't wait to give Jennifer Kennedy Dean's *Altar'd* the next read. And the next. Enlightening teaching, endearing transparency, and magnificently life-changing concepts keep the wow factor revved to the max from beginning to end. I don't think I'll ever see *altar* as a noun again. It's been totally "verbed" into a place of sweet action. *Altar'd* is a must-read. And a must-read again."

—*Rhonda Rhea, author of* How Many Lightbulbs Does It Take to Change a Person?

"Jennifer Kennedy Dean is one of our favorite guests to have on the show. Her love for Jesus and knowledge of God's Word consistently sets the stage for powerful and life-changing dialogue. Jennifer's new book, *Altar'd: Experience the Power of Resurrection*, invites readers on a journey to discover the transforming power of the risen Christ within a teachable heart. As Jennifer noted, 'The call to crucifixion is always to make a way for resurrection.' If you're done with status-quo and stagnant spirituality and you're willing to die to self that you might live more fully for Christ, take this book and take your time. Read one day at a time, let it get under your skin, in your bones, and into your heart. In due time you'll learn the glory, the power, and the promise of Christ within you."

—*Susie Larson, host of* Live the Promise with Susie Larson, *author of* The Uncommon

"The title alone is enough to grab you but the heart of the author and the passion that drives her will inspire you. Jennifer communicates profound biblical truths in a way that creates a hunger for more of the Jesus she loves. While she seeks to understand and live the altar'd life, you can't help but want to join her. What I've read and learned here has challenged and encouraged me. Thank you, Jennifer."

—*Jill Kelly, author of* New York Times *bestseller*
Without a Word: How a Boy's Unspoken Love Changed Everything

"This devotional is encouraging, inspirational, and challenging. An awesome reminder that the resurrection power of Christ is available to each of us, if we'll choose to live a life FULLY surrendered. *Altar'd* is a great book for anyone that wants to experience God's power in their life and ministry."

—*Matt Fry, lead pastor of C3 Church, Clayton, North Carolina*

OTHER NEW HOPE BOOKS BY
Jennifer Kennedy Dean

Life Unhindered! Five Keys to Walking in Freedom

Life-Changing Power in the Name of Jesus

Life-Changing Power in the Blood of Jesus

Live a Praying Life! Journal

Live a Praying Life! Open Your Life to God's Power and Provision

Live a Praying Life Bible Study

Live a Praying Life Leader Kit

The Power of Small: Think Small to Live Large

Pursuing the Christ: Prayers for Christmastime

Secrets Jesus Shared:
Kingdom Insights Revealed Through the Parables Leader Kit

Secrets Jesus Shared:
Kingdom Insights Revealed Through the Parables Bible Study

Set Apart: A 6-Week Study of the Beatitudes

jennifer kennedy dean

altar'd

30 DAYS OF TRANSFORMATION

EXPERIENCE THE POWER OF RESURRECTION

altar'd

EXPERIENCE
THE POWER OF
RESURRECTION

jennifer kennedy dean

NEW HOPE
PUBLISHERS

BIRMINGHAM, ALABAMA

New Hope® Publishers
P. O. Box 12065
Birmingham, AL 35202-2065
www.NewHopeDigital.com
New Hope Publishers is a division of WMU®.

Library of Congress Cataloging-in-Publication Data

Dean, Jennifer Kennedy.
  Altar'd : experience the power of resurrection / Jennifer Kennedy Dean.
    p. cm.
  ISBN 978-1-59669-331-9 (sc)
  1. Christian life--Meditations. 2. Flesh (Theology)--Meditations. I. Title.
  BV4509.5.D423 2012
  248.4--dc23
                        2011045842

ISBN-10: 1-59669-331-2
ISBN-13: 978-1-59669-331-9

N124138 • 0112 • 7M1

Original cover art concept design by Amber Waldeier, Liquid Blue Designs
liquidblue.us

Cover design: Michel Lê
Interior-page design: Glynese Northam

CONTENTS

INTRODUCTION

I can't trace how many years God has been teaching me about crucifixion of the flesh, and its consequent release of the Spirit's power. I have written about it — or at least mentioned it — in nearly every book I've ever written. I can see the seeds of the concept in my first book 20 years ago, and can trace its progression through subsequent books. I remember how it all started.

My husband went through a long period of unemployment. It was agony for me. The humiliation, the uncertainty, the fear, the loss of stuff, the tension. I tried every prayer secret I'd ever heard of to get God to come through. Fasting, begging, confessing, then confessing some more, getting others to pray . . . the list goes on.

On June 17, 1988, I wrote the following: "Reading Romans 12:1. What does it mean to be a living sacrifice? How do I die to myself? Just abstract concept to me, but I want to really know it. I want You to have all of me." Then I went back to whining and kvetching about my difficult situation that seemed to have no end.

A couple of weeks later, I seemed to have an *aha* moment. "Nothing I'm feeling right now could have origins in the Spirit. So only one other possibility? The flesh? Fear = flesh. Anger = flesh. Humiliation = flesh. I get that. So now what?" Without walking you with me through the years of prayer journals, suffice it to say that slowly, piece by piece, one baby step at a time, aha moment upon aha moment, I started to get it. God exposes flesh. I can choose to ignore that flesh and relegate it to its rightful crucifixion. I have come to call that a crucifixion moment. When that flesh succumbs to its prescribed death — crucifixion — then the power of resurrection takes its place. While I had been railing and wailing at God to take my problem away, He had been lovingly redefining the experience as a crucifixion that would lead to a resurrection. He was bringing flesh out of hiding and forcing it into the light where I could choose—yield to crucifixion, or resuscitate my flesh and keep on giving it power in my life.

God is about recreating. He doesn't just change you, He remakes you. The In-the-Beginning God is still the same Creator He has always been. He creates the same way. He brings form out of formlessness. He brings light out of darkness. He brings order out of chaos. He brings beauty out of ashes and fills up the empty places.

The recreating happens on the altar—at the Cross—where flesh goes to die.

In this 40-day devotional, I get to pull all the pieces together in one place. These concepts have revamped my life, and reoriented my view of every situation I encounter. For me, it has been a journey of deep-down recalibration—an uprooting of poisoned personality traits, an excavation of harmful responses on autopilot, an extraction of what is precious from what is worthless. I pray that I can adequately communicate this long and ongoing transforming journey I am on.

Altar'd

The noun *altar* is usually understood to be a place of worshipful offering. Something of value is offered up and released on the altar. The offerer relinquishes ownership and yields control to Another—a Power beyond.

Let's see what happens when we turn the noun *altar* into a verb. Altar our fear, our failure, our possessiveness, our need to control . . . all those things that hold us captive and keep us from running the race at full throttle.

Live in an *altar'd* state. Surrendered, yielded . . . free. Not offering sacrifice to appease a god who is vengeful; or to placate a god who is withholding; or to win the approval of a god who is angry. Live in an *altar'd* state to cooperate with the God who is committed to seeing you free of the toxic flesh that works against your freedom. Let the altar do its work in you, transforming fear to faith, worry to worship.

Each time that old pattern starts asserting itself in your thoughts, overlay it with the new reality: *I'm altar'd.*

On the altar, flesh is surrendered to crucifixion. Crucifixion is the prelude to resurrection. *Altar'd* living frees us to live in the power of His resurrection.

The Word Made Flesh

When Jesus came to live out His life on earth, the Word became flesh. He was the eternal Word of God manifested and made visible in the form of flesh. When the Word came to indwell us, He began a work of renewal, transforming our human flesh to become the lived-out Word. Once the Word was made flesh. Now, our flesh is being made the Word. We are not the messengers. We are the message. He is manifesting His message in our lives.

Day 1

THE NATURE OF FLESH

Since we will be using the word *flesh*, I want to take some time to work through *a* definition. In our main use of the word, flesh does not mean physical flesh. Succinctly, it refers to the parts of your human nature that are still operating on their own sin-producing power and not surrendered to the power of the indwelling Spirit. The word *flesh* as we will use it expresses itself through your body in actions, thoughts, words, attitudes, or responses, so the flesh includes the body, but the body is only the vehicle for the flesh to express itself.

A person without the indwelling Spirit of Jesus is all flesh in this sense. The person in whom Jesus has housed Himself and taken up residence has pockets of flesh still active. Like sleeper cells, they are activated by certain cues from the outside, but until activated, flesh might stay hidden. Hidden or disguised flesh is wreaking havoc inside like undetected cancer cells—free to destroy unchallenged.

We can't go exclusively by the word *flesh* in the biblical text because it is sometimes used to mean physical material—the corporeal body in which our personalities are contained. The act of translating from one language to another, like from Greek, Hebrew, or Aramaic into English, is more than simply replacing one word with another. It requires translating linguistic context and cultural meaning. Depending on what translation of the Bible you might be using, the same word or concept might be translated "flesh" (meaning soft body-tissue) one place and then "human nature," or "carnal nature," or "old man" in another. Or, the word might always be translated "flesh," but the textual setting interprets it as something more than the physical body. It is usually easy to tell the difference.

We will be talking about flesh as our unsurrendered sin nature. All of us still have active and uncrucified flesh. The process theologians call *sanctification* is the process of dragging flesh out of hiding, naming it what it is, and surrendering it to crucifixion. We are going to call it *altaring*. Living in an *altar'd* state, with flesh yielded.

Flesh Has a Tell

Though we can make all kinds of excuses for flesh, dress it up in religion and piety, flesh has a "tell." It *acts* like flesh. Whatever is born of flesh is flesh. Any action, attitude, emotion, word, or thought that has its roots in flesh is all flesh. Flesh and Spirit never act in harmony, One or the other, never both at the same time (Romans 8:4–8).

> *"Flesh gives birth to flesh, but the Spirit gives birth to spirit"* (JOHN 3:6).

> *"The Spirit gives life; the flesh counts for nothing. The words I have spoken to you are spirit and they are life"* (JOHN 6:63).

From these two statements Jesus made, we can glean several things about flesh. In John 3:6, Jesus is having His famous conversation with Nicodemus about being born of the Spirit. In this statement, He is talking about physical flesh, but the physical flesh that comes prepackaged with unredeemed human nature. The only thing that flesh can produce is flesh. Do you see in this statement the complete disconnect between flesh and God's Spirit? Either flesh or Spirit, but not both.

Then in John 6:63, Jesus says that flesh gets you nowhere, has no profit in it, conveys nothing of value. But, in contrast, Spirit gives life. Either/or, but not both. Jesus' words are spirit because their origins are in the Spirit. If it is born of the Spirit, then it is Spirit. If it is born of the flesh, then it is flesh.

So, what is the tell? How does flesh give itself away and reveal its nature?

Flesh is proud, possessive, demanding, grabby, angry, envious, wants to own and manage and manipulate and get its way. Flesh caters to its appetites—physical and emotional. Flesh is self-conscious. Flesh demands its own way. Flesh is all about the "I." I want. I will. I did. I feel.

Flesh's tell is not always easy to spot in ourselves. (By the way, don't try to spot it in others. That's not your job.) Flesh doesn't always look ugly on the surface. In fact, it cleans up very nicely sometimes. Flesh that has religious training can masquerade as all kinds of admirable qualities. Through this 40-day journey we'll learn how to identify flesh. We'll find our own flesh's tell, and then how to surrender it to crucifixion.

Flesh Versus Spirit

Flesh and Spirit cannot reach a compromise or form a peace treaty. The very presence of one eliminates the other. Like light and dark. Where it is dark, there is no light. Where it is light, there is no darkness. One cancels out the other.

> *"For the sinful nature [flesh] desires what is contrary to the Spirit, and the Spirit what is contrary to the sinful nature [flesh]. They are in conflict with each other"* (GALATIANS 5:17).

> *"Those who live according to the sinful nature [flesh] have their minds set on what that nature desires; but those who live in accordance with the Spirit have their minds set on what the Spirit desires"* (ROMANS 8:5).

With this in mind, let me reiterate: what does not come from the Spirit comes from the flesh.

When I started processing this in my life, it was a surprise to me how much of my energy and effort came from flesh. I had evaluated my life as pretty spiritual. I prayed, studied, and memorized the Scripture, told the truth, tried to be kind. I have quite a long list of proofs that I was very, very spiritual. Really spiritual.

I only had a limited way to categorize. Good or bad. Sin or not sin. It was a flesh-engaging, me-focused kind of activity. With all its spiritual overtones, still it put me at the center of my universe. It's a way of living that might sound humble and noble, and it was certainly meant that way. Only much later could I look back and see that flesh thinks only flesh can straighten flesh out, so flesh had better be vigilant.

Then I learned a new way to see. I learned about flesh and Spirit.

As we move through this journey, don't worry that you will have to live a life of either constant examination and self-flagellation or self-congratulation. You will be freed from that. You will be freed from trying to measure up and from chasing your flesh around with a foam bat, trying to get it under control but having no effect. Those days are over.

REFLECT

How much time do you spend feeling guilty and discouraged?

too much

In moments of harsh honesty, do you feel that you never quite measure up no matter how hard you try?

yes

Are you tired of trying to live the way you long to live?

it is tiring

FLIMFLAM FLESH

Flesh makes big promises. It entices you into its realm where it makes claims and gives you its word of honor that the happiness, or peace, or fulfillment you are looking for are right there. Then it fizzles. When you have put all your effort and all your trust and confidence in your flesh—when you've worked it and kneaded it and tried to shape it up—that's when it fails you.

One of two things is likely to happen. You make peace with your flesh. You say, "Nobody's perfect and I'm not under law, I'm under grace. I've got to quit judging myself and accept who I am." Go, flesh, go! You see, this has some truth in it. True, you are under grace. True, you need to stop living in state of condemnation. But Spirit will never make a pact with flesh to live in harmony, and your flesh's promise of peace will not be kept.

The second is that you will conclude that you are a hopeless case. You will live a pretend life to the best of your ability and never step out into the light. You'll find ways to hide and disguise the real you and live in fear of exposure. You will live a life of self-loathing.

Flesh hawks a cheap happiness that circumvents crucifixion. But, like all cheap imitations, it breaks down quickly and doesn't really do the job.

> *They dress the wound of my people*
> *as though it were not serious.*
> *'Peace, peace,' they say,*
> *when there is no peace.*
> (JEREMIAH 6:14)

If at First You Don't Succeed

Flesh is all about trying. Spirit is all about dying. Flesh says, "Try a little harder! You can do it!" Spirit says, "Die a little deeper. I can do it." Flesh lives by this motto: Believe in yourself! Spirit lives by this motto: Die to yourself.

Flesh receives input through the senses and from the factory preinstalled thought patterns passed down through generations of flesh. We're all born flesh. Flesh as in flesh-and-blood body, but also flesh as in our sinning nature at the controls. We come already wounded, because flesh's DNA has sin it. Our flesh has a bent toward following the inclinations of the flesh and so expressing that flesh through sinful acts and attitudes.

As the Scripture talks about flesh, there is no need to single out one person's flesh from another's. Flesh is flesh. It always acts like itself. In any generation, in any culture, in any situation flesh acts and thinks the same. I repeat: We come with flesh as our preloaded operating system running preloaded flesh programs.

We are wired to try harder. We resonate with calls to try harder. Why do you think that is? I think because the flesh is also programmed with a]need to feel in control. See this on display in the story of Naaman found in 2 Kings 5:1–14.

Resurrection from Crucifixion

Naaman. The very name had come to mean courage and strength to the people of Aram. Naaman was a national hero, a valiant warrior. Naaman had it all. But Naaman was a leper.

> *"Now Naaman was commander of the army of the king of Aram. He was a great man in the sight of his master and highly regarded, because through him the Lord had given victory to Aram. He was a valiant soldier, but he had leprosy"*
> (2 KINGS 5:1).

Naaman was living under a death sentence. His flesh was full of death.

A prophet in Samaria—a man named Elisha—an obscure, uncelebrated man of God might—just might—hold the key that would bring life out of Naaman's death.

Naaman surrounded himself with the trappings that announced his high position and set off for the humble dwelling place of the man of God. Met at Elisha's door, not by the humble prophet himself, but by the humble prophet's *servant*, Naaman hears the prescription for his ailment: "Go dip yourself in the Jordan River seven times."

Outraged, insulted, incredulous! Naaman refused to do such a degrading thing as to dip himself in the Jordan River seven times. There were better rivers back home! Where's the hand-waving and the shouting and the drama? Something to validate what an important man Naaman was!

> *"But Naaman went away angry and said, 'I thought that he would surely come out to me and stand and call on the name of the Lord his God, wave his hand over the spot and cure me of my leprosy. Are not Abana and Pharpar, the rivers of Damascus, better than any of the waters of Israel? Couldn't I wash in them and be cleansed?' So he turned and went off in a rage"* (2 Kings 5:11–12).

His servants knew him well. They had seen him perform feats in battle that had cemented his reputation for mettle and prowess. They knew how he viewed himself—a master and a winner. So, they knew how to appeal to him.

> *"Naaman's servants went to him and said, 'My father, if the prophet had told you to do some great thing, would you not have done it? How much more, then, when he tells you, "Wash and be cleansed"!'"* (2 Kings 5:13).

If only the God of Israel had required something daring. Something bold. Something only the great and mighty Naaman could do. That would have been easy.

Naaman had lived a life marked by uncommon courage. He had put his life at risk on the battlefield time and time again. But the hardest thing Naaman ever did was to dip himself in the Jordan River seven times. It was the death sentence for his pride, but it was the only way for Naaman to have life. The choice was his—life or death.

When Naaman emerged from the Jordan River the seventh time, he had the skin of a little child. You might say he'd been born again. He had passed from death to life. You might say his crucifixion had yielded a resurrection.

Living Out of Control

Our flesh likes to be in control. Of everything. In control of ourselves, in control of the people around us, in control of our circumstances, in control of other people's circumstances. Nothing will throw our flesh into a bigger revolt than when we realize we have to hand over control. It's a death blow to our pride.

No way around it. Out-of-control flesh is the secret to surrendering to the power of the Spirit. Remember, there will be no shared governing. Flesh or Spirit, but not both.

When you are experiencing frustration, anger, or bitterness because you can't get the people around you to act like you need them to act, you can call that flesh. When you are in a panic, or filled with resentment because you can't manipulate circumstances into order, you can call that flesh.

The impulse of our flesh is to try harder, manage more, enforce our will more stringently, maneuver and massage and finesse until we get everyone and everything straightened out and marching to our beat.

Some people's flesh comes on strong in a frontal assault. They use intimidation and demanding to try to line things up. Others do the manipulating from a stealth position, relying on their wiles and ability to play on either fears or emotions to get things lined up. It doesn't matter. Both patterns are equally deft at bringing all the death-bearing aspects of flesh into the situation. Whether dressed up to be sweet and winsome, or revealed as overbearing and forceful, flesh is flesh is flesh.

The reason that our flesh rises up and gives its all to make things fit its goals is because flesh promises that if everything and everyone would just do and be what we want them to do and be, then the happiness and peace that eludes us would be ours. Flimflam flesh. Big claims, no results. It gets you nowhere.

REFLECT

What people or circumstances in your life are exposing your flesh?

My husband & kids

Can you identify concretely ways you recognize flesh at work?

- trying to get a handle on everything
not letting God take control -
then when I can't - it is frustrating

" oh well" - not always can actually
not ever can I manage the outcome.

& my weight + excercise - I am afraid
that my flesh will

→ Do I ask God to control + guide
me
provide me opportunity for this?

Day 3
FLAILING FLESH

Are you getting a clear understanding of flesh? Have you started recognizing flesh in your life? Let's spend one more day clarifying what we mean by flesh in the way we are using it in this journey. Flesh means operating in the power of our own sin-soiled human nature.

I hear people refer to "the sins of the flesh," as if that is a category of sin separate from some other kind of sin. I think they usually mean sins that have to do with the body, like sexual immorality or substance abuse. The phrase seems to mean outward behaviors, or sins performed by the body.

Let me take issue with that use of the phrase. The flesh is more than the body. All sins are sins of the "flesh." Sin is a fruit that has a root called unrighteousness that grows in ground called flesh. We'll go into more detail about that later, but sin grows out of flesh. All sin has flesh as its starting point.

Sin diminishes you. That's what puts it in the category of sin. It is harmful to you. It gunks up the inner workings of your life and slows your progress. It creates a spiritual sludge that keeps your life from the fullness for which you were created. God hates sin because of what it does to you.

Flesh generates sin. Flesh nourishes the root that grows a fruit called sin. All sin is born out of flesh. Flesh can only reproduce flesh.

"Flesh gives birth to flesh, but the Spirit gives birth to spirit" (JOHN 3:6).

"The Spirit gives life; the flesh counts for nothing. The words I have spoken to you are spirit and they are life" (JOHN 6:63).

Flesh works hard, but gets nowhere. Flesh talks a good game, but comes up empty. Flesh flails and thrashes and gives the appearance of action, but ends up unable to produce life or power. The writer of Hebrews calls it "dead works" (Hebrews 9:14 NASB).

Using the ceremonial levitical laws and sacrifices of the Old Covenant as his setting, the writer of Hebrews is addressing Jewish Christians who have started going back to the old ways of obtaining renewed standing with God. They have started trusting their own efforts—performing rituals now rendered empty by the sacrifice of Christ on the Cross. What would the attraction be? Why would anyone, once freed from the onerous dictates of making sure that every sin was atoned for through his own efforts by bringing a satisfactory sacrifice and offering it on the altar, willingly return to the burdensome ritual? Tada! See flesh work. Even though it was harder; even though it was burdensome; even though it was costly, still it was under the control of the person who sinned. Flesh says: "I'll take care of everything. Yes, it will cost me. But I'm up to the task. When I offer that sacrifice, I'm the one doing it. I can look at it and say I did it. Then I would deserve my forgiveness." Effort that has its roots in flesh, no matter how well-intentioned or rule-following it may be, is dead work. Life will never come from it.

The Power of Death

Death is more than the absence of life; it is a power that operates in and through the flesh. Death is an active force that works in Adam's race to produce fruit, just as life works in the children of God to produce fruit.

> "The mind of sinful man [human nature or flesh] is death, but the mind controlled by the Spirit is life and peace; the sinful mind is hostile to God. It does not submit to God's law, nor can it do so. Those controlled by the sinful nature [flesh] cannot please God" (ROMANS 8:5–8).

> "For when we were controlled by the sinful nature [flesh], the sinful passions aroused by the law were at work in our bodies, so that we bore fruit for death" (ROMANS 7:5).

Flesh is powered by the force of death. Anything that is not life is death. Death is the "not life." "He who has the Son has life; he who does not have the Son of God does not have life" (1 John 5:12). May I paraphrase? He who does not have the indwelling Jesus has the "not life"—death.

If you are reading this book, my best guess is that you do have the indwelling Jesus. You do have life. But, we all have pockets of flesh still active because we keep them on automatic life support. We have areas in our lives that still run by flesh power. Every action, thought, attitude, or belief that grows out of that ground produces fruit for death.

Dead Fruit

So as not to be too esoteric, let me clarify what I mean by death in this context. Not physical death, but the state of being and the operating power that is anything other than Jesus, who is the Life. Anything other than Jesus, operating in you by the power of His Spirit, is death. At best, it produces nothing. At worst, it brings chaos and destruction.

Let's imagine a scenario. I'm going to make these characters up, but they will be based on reality. Imagine Jane, who does indeed have Jesus indwelling, and His present power has changed her life in many ways. For example, she no longer lies or misleads to make herself feel more acceptable to others. She used to enjoy gossiping about her neighbors, but no longer finds it pleasurable. In many areas of her personality Jane has experienced the crucifixion of her flesh that has set her free and now allows her to be a vessel through which Jesus can work.

But Jane is still a person with sin and still has pockets of flesh active in her personality. Jane has a teenaged daughter. We'll name her Mary. Mary is not a compliant teenager. Let's say that she has some tattoos and piercings, and that she has a combative relationship with her mother.

Jane is concerned about Mary on several levels. She honestly wants Mary to become the person God means for her to be for Mary's sake. Much of Jane's concern does revolve around her love for her daughter. But, truth be told, she also has a concern about what people think of Jane when they see Mary. Jane has always had trouble with her concern about what others might think of her. That's why she used to mislead, or why she found some relief in putting others down through gossip. Now that same pattern of flesh rears its head again, massaged into viability by daughter Mary and her tattoos.

Jane's flesh is convinced that if she can just get Mary to look and act and think like Jane thinks she should, all would be well. So she pulls out all the stops. Falls into patterns modeled for her for generations. She shames, she puts down, she compares Mary to other girls her age, she makes herself out to be a martyr. And what does she accomplish? Mary dies inside a little more. Their relationship dies a little more. Mary's sense of who she is gets anchored more strongly to her outward appearance. Mary believes her behaviors define her. Flesh gives birth to flesh. Dead works result in giving the "not life" more access. When Jane acts from her flesh, her actions bear fruit for death.

Here's the problem. Jane's flesh has responded to Mary's flesh. First, Jane needs to look past Mary's flesh. "Therefore from now on we recognize no man according to the flesh; even though we have known Christ according to the flesh, yet now we know Him thus no longer" (2 Corinthians 5:16 NASB). Paul is saying that at some point we responded to Christ from the perspective of our flesh, but we are past that. We realize that our response to Christ has to be from the Spirit because Christ is now glorified. Then Paul takes it a step further. Anyone who is in Christ is a brand-new creation. Since that newly created person is in Christ, that person responds through Christ, who has no sinning flesh. So, we don't interact with people based on flesh—our flesh responding to their flesh. Now we see right past their flesh and respond through the Spirit.

REFLECT

Do you recognize any ways that your flesh is responding to someone else's flesh?

✱ Being late, acting up → what others will think
  Hurpues hurts not acknowledge

Do you see dead works bearing fruit for death?

(A not supporting the kids
  → let God define them.

FACTS ABOUT FLESH

F lesh is sin's ground zero. Flesh is the platform from which sin is launched. In flesh, sin finds a welcoming environment where it can root and flourish. Sin is an active component that is fueled by flesh. However I describe it, it means the same thing. Flesh and sin work in tandem. Flesh expresses itself through sin. So, if we want to understand flesh, then we have to bring sin into focus.

Let's establish some vocabulary for discussing these concepts. Over the years of my study and search for answers, I've boiled down a few definitions that work for me. In Scripture, the wording will depend on which translation you use, but it seems to me that context clarifies the meaning of these words.

Flesh. We've been defining flesh all along. Let me add one thing here. In the first human, flesh was neutral until the act of sin corrupted flesh by cutting it off from the life of God. Since Adam, humans have been born with corrupted flesh predisposed to sin. All flesh sins and falls short of the glory of God. Jesus, born as a human, had uncorrupted flesh which remained uncorrupted through every testing. He operated in a sinless body and through a sinless personality.

Sin and sins. Often the use of the word *sin* will reference the principle of sin, the operating power of sin in the unredeemed human nature. The word *sins* (or the singular *sin* when referring to a behavior) most often refers to sinful actions and behaviors. Because of the power of sin, we commit sins. Sin produces sins. We are all born members of Adam's race with a sin nature, and therefore we all sin.

Born again. At the moment that we enter into relationship with God through His Son Jesus Christ, a transaction occurs that is so complete and so utterly transformational that Jesus referred to it as being born again. That little phrase is replete with all the elements of our transforming salvation. He is not suggesting that a *second* you is born, but that a *new* you is born. The old you is gone—dead and buried—and a new you—a freshly minted, brand-new you—has been born. For a new you to be born, the old you has to die. Paul put it in these words: "I have been crucified with Christ and I no longer live, but Christ lives in me" (Galatians 2:20). We'll keep adding to that concept as we go along.

Flesh's Folly

In the beginning, God created mankind to be the image of Himself. He created our human personality. It is His wonderful, ingenious, amazing design. The human personality—thinking, willing, creating, desiring, reasoning, relating—is not evil or wrong in itself. In fact, God is restoring the human personality to be what He intended it to be: the vehicle through which He expresses Himself in the world.

The Creator designed us to have needs. He built needs into the blueprint so that those needs would be His entry points into our lives. He configured our needs so that they would be an exact match to His provision, as if the two were interlocking parts, fitting together hand-in-glove.

Flesh takes those God-designed needs and tries to find their fulfillment on its own, from something or someone other than God. To see this in operation, let's examine the beginnings of corrupted flesh.

The First Flesh

The creation account is all about freedom. It's odd that we often focus on the one single restriction rather than the amazing freedom. Imagine being Adam and Eve. A whole world just for you. Enjoy! Learn! You can do anything you desire, anything you see is yours. Just one caveat: If you eat the fruit of this one tree—just one tree out of the whole creation—you will die, for sure. You can enjoy your extravagant freedom—a freedom that is protected by the one lone constraint.

Genesis 3:1–24 tells the story we call the Fall. This is when flesh (human nature) became corrupted. Until this incident, the man and the woman had what we are calling flesh, but it was in its right alignment—looking to God and responding to His voice and obeying His protective decree. Let's revisit the familiar story and see what it tells us about flesh.

Now the serpent was more crafty than any of the wild animals the Lord God had made. He said to the woman, "Did God really say, 'You must not eat from any tree in the garden'?"

The woman said to the serpent, "We may eat fruit from the trees in the garden, but God did say, 'You must not eat fruit from the tree that is in the middle of the garden, and you must not touch it, or you will die.'"

"You will not surely die," the serpent said to the woman. "For God knows that when you eat of it your eyes will be opened, and you will be like God, knowing good and evil."

When the woman saw that the fruit of the tree was good for food and pleasing to the eye, and also desirable for gaining wisdom, she took some and ate it. She also gave some to her husband, who was with her, and he ate it (GENESIS 3:1–6).

I am taken by the tempter's approach. "Did God really say, 'You must not eat from *any tree* in the garden'?" He takes a kernel of the truth and grows a lie from it. Framing the question so that it suggests that God is all about restraint and limitations; hinting that if God has His way, the woman will be denied something that would make her happy and fulfilled. Planting the germ of an idea that there might be some source outside of God.

Flesh falls for the misdirection. Don't look at the freedom, look at the prohibition. Dissatisfaction, once introduced, finds that flesh is fertile ground. The text seems to say that though she had looked at the tree many times before and knew exactly where it was, she had never seen it as an object of desire. She had never considered disobeying God. On that pivotal day, instead of seeing the tree as God saw it — protection — she saw the tree as the tempter defined it — restriction.

I think it is here, even before the act, that flesh was corrupted. Right here, when the woman considered the possibility that something other than God might meet her needs and fulfill her desires, flesh fell. Sin took advantage and sins followed.

REFLECT

Be brutally honest. In your heart of hearts, do you see God as withholding and restrictive?

Do your thoughts and habits prove that you believe that "my God will meet all your needs according to his glorious riches in Christ Jesus" (Philippians 4:19)?

Day 5
FLESH BLOOMS

T he nature of corrupted flesh comes into clear focus. Flesh flowers into full bloom as the woman considers the forbidden tree from a new perspective. Before, she had looked at it and said to herself, "That will harm me." This day she looked at it and said to herself, "That will enhance me." We don't know how long Adam and Eve lived in the garden before this fateful day, but for all the days preceding they had chosen time and again to obey. They saw the tree, but they did not eat from it. On this day, though, the need and desire that had always driven them to God was turned away from God and toward another source.

"When the woman saw that the fruit of the tree was *good for food* and *pleasing to the eye,* and also *desirable for gaining wisdom,* she took and ate it" (Genesis 3:6; emphasis added). Keep those words in mind.

Here is how the Scripture describes all the trees that God made for Adam and Eve to enjoy: "Now the Lord God had planted a garden in the east, in Eden; and there he put the man he had formed. And the Lord God made all kinds of trees grow out of the ground—trees that were *pleasing to the eye* and *good for food*" (Genesis 2:8–9; emphasis added). Do you see the echo of the phrases?

The deceiver appealed to her legitimate desires (a delight to the eyes) and played on her God-given needs (good for food) to lead her to believe that she could find a way to satisfy those needs and desires on her own (desirable for gaining wisdom). She could be wise herself instead of looking to wisdom Himself (1 Corinthians 1:24, 30). *She could be her own source.* Ultimately the temptation to which the first Adam fell was this: You can be your own source. You can do for yourself that which God has promised to do for you. You can obtain for yourself that which God has promised to give you. You can be like God.

Do you see how flesh works? Flesh tries to get its needs met outside of God. "If I can make this relationship be what I want it to be; if I can make people respond to me like I want them to respond; if I can prove my worth by owning enough stuff, or acquiring a high enough position, or having a sterling reputation. . . ." On and on with no end to the list. Flesh has to work hard because managing and controlling your life and the lives of those around you is more than a full-time job. Flesh never rests.

The garden God had designed for humans to inhabit was a place of rest. The work was already done; all that needed was tending. Later, we'll talk about how God restores that rest to His people. For now, realize that when flesh fell for the deception, flesh's promise proved false, as it always will. Flesh doesn't know the word *enough*. Whatever it is that your flesh has fastened its hope on, you will never get there. You won't ever have enough, or be enough. The people you are trying to squeeze love from will never give you enough. The accomplishment you thought would finally prove your value, after a momentary high, is soon passé—yesterday's news. Life is tiring, stressful, draining. Just when you think you're almost *there*—*there* moves.

Flesh Is Powered by Death

Remember that death is a force. It is the "not life." Consider that when God told Adam and Eve that when (as soon as) they ate from the forbidden tree they would surely (without question, definitely) die, they had no experiential knowledge of what death was. Death had never occurred in their experience. They had no concrete concept of death.

The first death occurred when, to cover their sinful state, God killed an animal and used its skin as a covering. So when you think about this account, do not imagine that they had a clear idea of the "death" they were admitting into their experience. This is one of the reasons that they fell so easily into sin. They did not know what death was.

At the moment that flesh flowered into sinful action, the power of death took the place of life. Adam and Eve—archetype of all humanity until the end of time—were designed to be life containers, but became death containers. Where life was meant to flow, death flowed instead. Death began. Physical death is the ultimate expression of the power of death, but not the whole picture.

In the material realm, scientists divide things into classifications—organic or inorganic; living or nonliving. Organisms cannot change classifications. The law of biogenesis says life comes from life. A nonliving organism cannot produce a living organism. A rock, for example, will never produce a flower. What is nonliving—lifeless—cannot become living. That which is born inorganic is inorganic; that which is born organic is organic. An organism cannot pass from death to life. An organism cannot change its essential nature and become what it is not.

In the spiritual realm, only Jesus is life.

> *"In him was life, and that life was the light of men"* (JOHN 1:4).

> *"For as the Father has life in himself, so he has granted the Son to have life in himself"* (JOHN 5:26).

> *"I am the way and the truth and the life"* (JOHN 14:6).

> *"So that they may take hold of the life that is truly life"* (1 TIMOTHY 6:19).

> *"The life appeared; we have seen it and testify to it"* (1 JOHN 1:2).

> *"He who has the Son has life; he who does not have the Son of God does not have life"* (1 JOHN 5:12).

Everything else is flesh—progressive death. In the spiritual realm, the two classifications are flesh or Spirit. That which is born of the flesh is flesh; that which is born of the Spirit is Spirit. Life is only in the Son, so only the Son can impart life. Life must come from life—spiritual biogenesis. Only the person who has the Son has life. He who has the Son has life; he who has not the Son has "not life."

A person without the indwelling present Jesus is described in the Word as dead.

> *"As for you, you were dead in your transgressions and sins, in which you used to live when you followed the ways of this world and of the ruler of the kingdom of the air, the spirit who*

is now at work in those who are disobedient. All of us also lived among them at one time, gratifying the cravings of our sinful nature and following its desires and thoughts. Like the rest, we were by nature objects of wrath. But because of his great love for us, God, who is rich in mercy, made us alive with Christ even when we were dead in transgressions" (EPHESIANS 2:1–5).

"When you were dead in your sins and in the uncircumcision of your sinful nature, God made you alive with Christ. He forgave us all our sins" (COLOSSIANS 2:13).

Flesh can only produce more flesh. Flesh is powered by death. "When you were slaves to sin, you were free from the control of righteousness. What benefit did you reap at that time from the things you are now ashamed of? Those things result in death!" (ROMANS 6:20–21).

Just as the Spirit produces fruit in the life of those in whom He lives, so death produces fruit in the lives of those in whom it lives. "For when we were controlled by the sinful nature, the sinful passions aroused by the law were at work in our bodies, so that we *bore fruit for death*" (Romans 7:5). The power of flesh and death produces "dead works."

REFLECT

Have you identified the way(s) your flesh is trying to find satisfaction and validation from something outside of God?

Do you recognize areas in your life where your God-given desires and needs are driving your flesh?

- control
- peace

GOOD-FOR-NOTHING FLESH

This seems to be my refrain: Flesh gets you nowhere. It never, ever accomplishes what you thought it would. Yet, there it is. Flesh, flesh, and more flesh. And your flesh has tried to tame your flesh for years. What to do?

It's time to see what remedy the Scripture gives to the flesh problem. Today I want to give you the big picture, then we will drill down and look at the details and let the Spirit apply it to the minutia of your life, because that is where flesh has its hold. Life is made up of millions and millions of moments, punctuated by a few big upheavals. When we deal with our flesh in the dailyness of living life, then we'll be ready to head into life's few big moments in an altar'd state. Flesh out of the way; Spirit's power unfurled.

To Know Him in the Power of His Resurrection

The flesh problem has only one remedy. It has to be surrendered to crucifixion. It can't be dressed up or cleaned up. It has to die a messy, bloody, merciless crucifixion death.

> *"For we know that our old self was crucified with him so that the body of sin might be done away with, that we should no longer be slaves to sin—because anyone who has died has been freed from sin"* (ROMANS 6:6–7).

> *"I have been crucified with Christ and I no longer live, but Christ lives in me"* (GALATIANS 2:20).

"May I never boast except in the cross of our Lord Jesus Christ, through which the world has been crucified to me, and I to the world" (GALATIANS 6:14).

"For you died, and your life is now hidden with Christ in God" (COLOSSIANS 3:3).

The good news is this: a crucifixion is the prelude to a resurrection. Resurrection power—the power of Christ who overcame the last enemy, death—is the endgame. The path to resurrection passes through crucifixion. Like Paul, "I want to know Christ and the power of his resurrection and the fellowship of sharing in his sufferings, becoming like him in his death, and so, somehow, to attain to the resurrection from the dead" (Philippians 3:10–11). To experience the power of His Resurrection here and now. To be lifted out of the state of death my flesh lives in.

As we go on, we will examine in detail how to surrender flesh to crucifixion. We'll get to the nitty-gritty particulars and not leave it as a heady theory. Right now, I want to outline it in broad strokes and make sure we understand the concept before we put it under the microscope. We need to see the whole picture before we zoom in and isolate the pixels. So, stick with me as we keep working through the overall concept. It will give us the foundation on which to ground the specifics.

The Scriptures you just looked at that clearly state the principle of crucifixion of the flesh also indicate that it is a finished work. Christ's crucifixion is your flesh's crucifixion. I *have been crucified* with Christ. Our old self *was crucified* with Him. All done. Past tense.

For clarity, let me emphasize that it is not your personality that died with Christ. He is not trying to obliterate the you He so carefully designed. He is targeting the power and rule of flesh over your personality. He wants you to be free to be the beautiful, free, exuberant person He created you to be. As we move forward in talking about crucifixion of flesh, understand that He is not trying to turn you into some kind of automaton. He is working to free you of the dead weight of your flesh so your God-designed personality can flourish.

Your flesh—not your personality—has been crucified with Christ. How can that be? After pondering this for many years, here is the explanation that I find satisfying. Perhaps it will communicate it to you too.

1. God does not see in the context of linear time, but instead knows and sees everything at once. He knows the end from the beginning. He sees every step along the way. Past, present, future are all the same to Him.

2. God prepared our salvation before the first sin was ever committed and had the answer ready before the need arose. John, in his revelation of heaven, saw "the Lamb that was slain from the creation of the world" (Revelation 13:8).

3. God has always seen that you would come to faith in Christ and be a beneficiary of His death, resurrection, and indwelling life: "Your eyes saw my unformed body. All the days ordained for me were written in your book before one of them came to be" (Psalms 139:16).

4. At the moment in linear time when Jesus died on the Cross, God saw you in Him. He knew that you would accept Christ's death that paid for your sins, and His indwelling life that cleanses you of unrighteousness. He knew that your flesh, little by little, would experience its crucifixion. He can see as finished what we can see as in process.

5. What God sees is the reality. What I perceive in my limited way of seeing is partial and out of focus and is not the best way of judging reality. If God calls it finished, then I need to embrace that reality and consider it finished.

So, when my flesh asserts itself, it is really already crucified. It doesn't have any life of its own. Then why is it active? As I see it, it's because I have it on automatic life support.

Years ago there was a movie called *Weekend at Bernie's*. In the movie, two young executives were invited to their boss's beach house. Before they arrived, their boss was murdered by a mobster. The two young men pretend Bernie, their boss, is still alive. They move him around and get behind him to animate him so that he seems to be living. The whole movie is taken up with their deceit and the mobster's frustration trying to kill Bernie, who, of course, is already dead. This silly movie plot reminds me of how we try to animate our flesh, even though it is dead. What hard work! Dragging around a body of death!

To Know Him in the Fellowship of His Sufferings

We "were baptized into his death" (Romans 6:3). We "have been united with him like this in his death" (Romans 6:5). The key is His death. Jesus has already died the death and we are united with Him in *His* death.

In every instance, dying to flesh is clearing the way to life—real life, abundant life. "The death he died, he died to sin once for all; but the life he lives, he lives to God" (Romans 6:10). Since we are united with Him in His death, we, too, die to sin and experience being more alive to God. Each time we surrender one more pocket of flesh to His crucifixion, we die to sin. If you recall the definitions we laid out, *sin* refers to sin as an operating principle that produces sinful behaviors. Since flesh is where sin finds nourishment, when another pocket of flesh dies, sin has no foothold there and those sins cease to be. It is an ongoing process, but a steady progression.

Every time you surrender flesh to crucifixion, you are opening the way for resurrection. When the supernatural Godward life of Jesus rushes in to fill the space left vacant by old, rotten flesh that has been crucified, the power of His resurrection is your new experience. His life is on display where flesh has been displaced. The power of His death works *in* you, so the power of His life can work *through* you.

> "We always carry around in our body the death of Jesus, so that the life of Jesus may also be revealed in our body. For we who are alive are always being given over to death for Jesus' sake, so that his life may be revealed in our mortal body. So then, death is at work in us, but life is at work in you"
> (2 Corinthians 4:10–12).

REFLECT

What does it mean to you right now that you have been crucified with Christ? Take a few minutes to let it soak in until you can embrace it as your new reality.

THE POWER OF THE CROSS

T he Cross of Christ stands as the point of separation between the old person powered by death-driven corrupted flesh, and the new creation, powered by the very Spirit who raised Jesus from the dead. At the moment you embrace the Cross, you receive its power into your life—a power that is eternally and continually working. Paul says that "death is at work in us." At work in us now. Doing ongoing work. Doing present work. A. B. Simpson says,

> "We may not preach a crucified Saviour without being also crucified men and women. It is not enough to wear an ornamental cross as a pretty decoration. The cross that Paul speaks about was burned into his very flesh, was branded into his being, and only the Holy Spirit can burn the true cross into our innermost life."

The death that Jesus died on the Cross cannot be—and need not be—repeated. Only He is able to die for our sins, having no sins of His own to die for. The priests of the Old Testament, which were foreshadows of our Great High Priest, had to offer sacrifices first for their own sins, then for the sins of the people. But Jesus had no sins to be atoned for, and He alone is able to bear our sins on our behalf. The writer of Hebrews explained it:

> "Unlike the other high priests, he does not need to offer sacrifices day after day, first for his own sins, and then for the sins of the people. He sacrificed for their sins once for all when he offered himself" (HEBREWS 7:27).

As we surrender our corrupted flesh to His crucifixion, and as His death works in us, we are not repeating the atoning work of the Cross. That is done, completed, finished. Instead, we are letting the power of the Cross work out the crucifixion of our flesh. It is not a cross of punishment that works in us. The Cross did its work of punishment on the body of Jesus. It is the Cross that is freeing us from the confines and the distortions and the limitations of our sin nature. It is not restriction, but freedom. It is, in fact, the only hope of being all that we were created to be.

God designed the eternal cadence and it is built into creation at its crux. Life emerges out of death. The seed that falls into the ground to die to produce a harvest. The branch that is pruned so that it can bear more fruit. The beautiful colors of fall, ushering in the very death that will culminate in the springtime resurrection.

Living altar'd means surrendering to the death from which life comes. The Cross is the only place where flesh can go to die.

Flesh's Design

Flesh is designed to misdirect. Flesh will work hard to direct your gaze somewhere other than the Cross. Failing that, flesh will attempt to distort your view of the Cross. Make it seem ugly and harsh instead of life-giving and redemptive and tender.

I have something of a hobby, I guess you would call it, of reading books and articles and blogs by people who grew up in strong Christian homes, but as adults rejected their belief in Jesus. Their stories seem to have several common themes, but central to most is the theme of always trying to please a God who could not be pleased. They felt burdened and ashamed—always trying to measure up. They fell for a misdirection.

You know how a magician's tricks work. He depends on the fact that our minds can only focus on one thing at a time. He uses his skills to draw the focus of his audience where he wants it, so that he can do something else where his audience is not looking. The end result is that a lie appears to be the truth. He appears to have accomplished something by magic that was really done by trickery. It is very convincing.

This is what our flesh will try to induce in us. A misdirected focus. If flesh can keep you focused on your sin instead of His grace, then the myth of a rigid, angry god seems absolutely true. If your flesh can misdirect your focus away from the reality of the Cross, and keep your attention on your best effort, then the perception of a demanding, harsh god appears grounded in reality.

Our flesh operates by misdirection. Flesh never changes its ways. In us, it is always trying to pull our attention away from the beautiful Cross, where our freedom is to be found. It is always trying to keep us focused on our own failings, or our own fleeting successes, redefining the Cross as vindictive and vengeful and fearsome.

The Cross is a living power working in our lives to eradicate the flesh that holds us captive and stunts our growth. It has nothing to do with our ability to follow rules.

"May I never boast except in the cross of our Lord Jesus Christ, through which the world has been crucified to me, and I to the world. Neither circumcision nor uncircumcision (i.e., outward adherence) means anything; what counts is a new creation" (Galatians 6:14–15). If the Cross is working on the inside, then the evidence will show up on the outside. If, however, the flesh is working hard at conforming the outside, it will wear you out and discourage you. Flesh-produced outward changes that started out looking shiny and beautiful will fail the test of perseverance. It won't be lasting change. What counts is a new creation, transformed from the inside out. Not a spiffed-up old creation. The only way to live is to live altar'd.

REFLECT

Have you ever fallen for flesh's misdirection?

Take the time to refocus on the power of the Cross.

OUT WITH THE OLD, IN WITH THE NEW

"If anyone is in Christ, he is a new creation; the old has gone, the new has come!" (2 CORINTHIANS 5:17).

"You were taught, with regard to your former way of life, to put off your old self, which is being corrupted by its deceitful desires; to be made new in the attitude of your minds; and to put on the new self, created to be like God in true righteousness and holiness" (EPHESIANS 4:22–24).

"He told them this parable: 'No one tears a patch from a new garment and sews it on an old one. If he does, he will have torn the new garment, and the patch from the new will not match the old. And no one pours new wine into old wineskins. If he does, the new wine will burst the skins, the wine will run out and the wineskins will be ruined. No, new wine must be poured into new wineskins. And no one after drinking old wine wants the new, for he says, "The old is better"'" (LUKE 5:36–39).

T he key to getting rid of the old is letting in the new. I think we will have to state it this way: in with the new, out with the old. The power of living in an altar'd state comes from the indwelling life that flows forcefully, dislodging ingrown stubborn flesh and flushing flesh away in its wake. Until the new has come, the old is right at home. Nothing challenges its mastery or disturbs its environment. Flesh is king until it is dethroned and overthrown by the King.

We come then to the mainspring that sets the whole crucifixion-resurrection process in motion and keeps it moving: the indwelling, present life of Jesus.

In the beginning, God created the human being from the dust of the ground. Made him out of earth. He shaped and molded all the body parts until the human had everything he needed to operate in earth's environment. He had all the body parts and organs necessary for navigating earth. But he was not a finished product. He had the potential to live, but he had no life force. He was inanimate, no more alive than the dust and clay of which he was formed. An empty container. A vessel ready to be filled.

Then the Creator breathed His own breath into the human's nostrils, and the human was filled with life. The life breath of the Creator gave life to the created. The vessel now had an identity: he was a life container. What defines a vessel is whatever the vessel holds. Man became a living being—a vessel defined by the indwelling life of the Creator. He derived his life directly from the breath of God. Here stood God's pattern for perfection: a human with a body fitted for traversing earth, but filled with the life of heaven.

Then the famous fall. The only life force the human had ever experienced was withdrawn and where life had been, death took its place. The human was now powered by death. They who had been life containers were now death containers. Death began to work its work in them. Sin as an operating power had a new home. The power of sin began to produce the presence of sin in man's behavior.

When death and sin found their way into the human's soul, they produced the "old man" that Paul talks about. Decaying, dying, rotten—old. When the first humans reproduced, they reproduced after their own kind. Death ruled and "old men" were born into the line of Adam.

In Romans 5:12 we read that "sin entered the world through one man, and death through sin, and in this way death came to all men, because all sinned." Imagine that from my father I had inherited a genetic disorder that would mean my certain death. I might say, "Death came into my world through one man." Then imagine that I had passed that same fatal disorder on to my children, who passed it on to their children. Generations down the line, my descendants would still be saying, "Death came to me through one man."

The Birth of Hope

"For just as through the disobedience of the one man the many were made sinners, so also through the obedience of the one man the many will be made righteous" (ROMANS 5:19).

Aren't you glad that God plans ahead? Before the problem occurred, the solution was in place. God immediately set the plan in motion that would reverse the first Adam's actions and restore the original design. The eternal Son wrapped Himself in flesh and Mary's womb became the portal by which heaven entered earth. The Last Adam—Jesus—was born into the chaos and rubble death's reign had produced and began the walk that would win back what Adam lost.

In Romans 5:14, Adam is called *"a pattern of the one to come."* In 1 Corinthians 15:45, Jesus is called *"the last Adam."*

For the first time since the first Adam, there stood a man as God intended humans to be: in a body suited for earth, but filled and animated by the life of heaven. Like the first Adam, He would reproduce after His kind, opening the way to Spirit birth. People born in the line of the first Adam could be born again in the line of Jesus.

The last Adam would retrace the steps of the original Adam and, at each step, win the battle Adam lost. He would regain the ground Adam forfeited.

Let's look at the temptation accounts of the original Adam and the last Adam.

The first Adam was tempted at each level of his humanity—body, soul, and spirit.

From Genesis 3:1–6. What three things did Eve, the female human, see about the fruit of the forbidden tree? "When the woman saw that the fruit of the tree was good for food and pleasing to the eye, and also desirable for gaining wisdom, she took and ate it" (Genesis 3:6).

I believe she saw that it was good for food: an appeal to her body. She saw that it was pleasing to the eye: an appeal to her soul or personality. She saw that it was desirable for gaining wisdom: an appeal to her spirit. The tempter had said that if she were wise she would be "like God, knowing good and evil" (Genesis 3:5). This was the same desire that had been Lucifer's downfall: "I will make myself like the Most High" (Isaiah 14:14). This third attraction, then, was an appeal to her spiritual nature, by which she knew to worship and obey only God. She could be her own source—her own life force.

The forbidden tree was the Tree of the Knowledge of Good and Evil. You might think, "Wouldn't it make more sense to say that the fruit of the tree would cause them to know evil? After all, they already knew good." Did they know good? Some things you can only know by their opposites. You can only know light if you know dark. You can only know up if you know down. Unless they knew evil, they would not know good. They just knew what was. They did not recognize it as "good" until they came to know evil. So even though the fruit of the only tree forbidden her appealed to perfectly legitimate desires—the desire for food and the delight in beauty—it ultimately led to spiritual downfall. Her good desires were the openings through which temptation entered and brought sin. Ultimately the temptation to which the first Adam fell was this: You can be your own source. You can be like God.

The last Adam was tempted at each level of his humanity—body, soul, and spirit.

Matthew 4:3–11 records three temptations. The last Adam, Jesus, in His earth body, had the same openings the first Adam had. He had a human soul or personality (mind, will, and emotions). He had a human body. Satan's most direct assault on Him, in the desert following His baptism, took the same path as the tempter's assault on the first Adam. I would argue each level of His humanity was tested—body, soul, and spirit. Satan was looking for an opening.

1. **Tell these stones to become bread**—an appeal to His body.

2. **Throw Yourself off the highest point of the Temple and let the angels rescue you in the sight of everyone. Prove Yourself to them the easy way**—an appeal to His soul. It made a certain kind of sense and was an appeal to His mind. "What a good way to gather the people to Myself!" It was an appeal to His emotions. He could save both Himself and the people He loved great pain by short-circuiting the process. It appealed to His will. He desired for the people He came to save to see the truth and turn to Him.

3.I will give you all the kingdoms of the world if you will just bow down and worship me—an appeal to His spirit. It is His destiny that He will possess all the kingdoms of the world. All He had to do was worship one other than the Father and that which was rightfully His would be in His possession now.

In each case, the tempter appealed to Jesus' legitimate and right desires and needs. Each thing that the enemy dangled before Jesus was in line with God's desires for Him. God desired to meet Jesus' physical needs. He lived in a body that required food and it was God's desire that Jesus' body would be nourished. God desired that people would recognize Jesus as the Messiah and would come to Him. It was God's desire—had always been the plan—that Jesus would rule over the kingdoms of the world. The tempter wanted to convince Jesus to use His own independent resources to get His needs met. He wanted Jesus to take over and "do God's will" in His own power. He wanted Jesus to be His own source.

Jesus kept His flesh uncorrupted and won the victory. He overcame the enemy. When He comes to take up residence in us, He brings the victory with Him. His overcoming life flows through us like the vine's life flows through the branch. Everything about the DNA of the vine is communicated into, then through, the branch.

REFLECT

Can you identify the arena of your person where the tempter is enticing you to step out into flesh and be your own self-dependent source?

Be present to the Presence and let His overcoming life flow there. Lean into the Overcomer. Altar your flesh.

INSIDE OUT

T he plan was always the indwelling life of Christ, present in believers. In the beginning, the in-breathing of God imparted life to the human. Before His ascension, after His resurrection, John reports this: "Again Jesus said, 'Peace be with you! As the Father has sent me, I am sending you.' And with that he breathed on them and said, 'Receive the Holy Spirit'" (John 20:21–22).

First Adam—body of earth filled with the life of heaven. Last Adam—body of earth filled with the life of heaven. Humans as God had designed them to be. Now, believers—body of earth filled with the life of heaven. The divine design for humans is that they will be filled and fueled by the indwelling present Jesus.

Being united with Christ does not eliminate your free will. You are you and Jesus is Jesus. "I am the vine; you are the branches." Like the original humans, you will choose moment by moment whether to lean into Jesus or trust your flesh. You will decide whether or not you will live in an altar'd state. But knowing how close Jesus is—in all His power and His readiness to step in and take over every burden or situation—will change the way you live the minutes of your days.

Look again at Paul's famous words recorded in Galatians 2:20. "I have been crucified with Christ and I no longer live, but Christ lives in me. The life I live in the body, I live by faith in the Son of God, who loved me and gave himself for me." Paul acknowledges that, though his flesh or old man died with Christ, he is still living a life in his body. He chooses every minute to live that life with the confidence that the Lord Jesus is able to express Himself through the body and personality of Paul. He chooses to live out his life in an altar'd state, with his flesh surrendered to its crucifixion and his spirit alive to the presence of Jesus. Present to the Presence.

"I live by faith in the Son of God, who loved me and gave himself for me." When we live in dependence on the indwelling Jesus, then Jesus can be counted on to make use of His own created design that allows our personalities to be a conduit for His mind, will, and emotions. He set things up in the beginning to work like that. I can be the willing vessel through whom the living Lord Jesus acts and thinks. When I live by faith *in* Jesus, I live by the faith *of* Jesus. Jesus expresses His own faith through me when I rest the weight of my personality on Him. Lean in.

From inside, He is spilling over into you, then spilling over through you to the world around you. He is transforming you from the inside out, not like a drill sergeant shouting orders from the outside, but by being Himself in you. The living indwelling Jesus is involved in a restoration project. From the time He makes you His home, He begins to restore your soul—your personality—bringing it to its intended purpose, which is to be a reflection of His glory. From inside, He is pouring Himself into your mind, your will, and your emotions. These are the three aspects of our personalities that the Scripture identifies as transformed by Christ.

MIND

> *"The mind controlled by the Spirit is life and peace"*
> (ROMANS 8:6).

> *"Do not conform any longer to the pattern of this world, but be transformed by the renewing of your mind. Then you will be able to test and approve what God's will is—his good, pleasing and perfect will"* (ROMANS 12:2).

> *"We have the mind of Christ"* (1 CORINTHIANS 2:16).

> *"Be made new in the attitude of your minds"*
> (EPHESIANS 4:23–24).

> *"No one knows the thoughts of God except the Spirit of God. We have not received . . . the Spirit who is from God, that we may understand what God has freely given us"*
> (1 CORINTHIANS 2:11–12).

WILL

> *"It is God who works in you to will and to act according to his good purpose"* (PHILIPPIANS 2:13).

> *"If you remain in me and my words remain in you, ask whatever you wish, and it will be given you"* (JOHN 15:7).

The powerful presence of Christ in you is recreating your desires to match His.

EMOTIONS

> *"God has poured out his love into our hearts by the Holy Spirit, whom he has given us"* (ROMANS 5:5).

> *"For Christ's love compels us"* (2 CORINTHIANS 5:14).

Formation Through Transformation

Will I disappear? Will my personality be obliterated so that I march in lockstep with millions of other Christ followers, each indistinguishable from the other? Absolutely not. In fact, it will be just the opposite. C. S. Lewis addresses this question in his book *Mere Christianity*.

> To become new [people] means losing what we now call "ourselves." Out of ourselves, into Christ, we must go. His will is to become ours and we are to think His thoughts, to "have the mind of Christ" as the Bible says. And if Christ is one, and if He is thus to be "in" us all, shall we not be exactly the same? It certainly sounds like it; but in fact it is not so.
>
> But I will try two very imperfect illustrations which may give a hint of the truth. Imagine a lot of people who have always lived in the dark. You come and try to describe to them what light is like. You might tell them that if they come into the light that same light would fall on them all and they would all reflect it and thus become what we call visible. Is it not quite possible that they would imagine

that, since they were all receiving the same light, and all reacting to it in the same way (i.e., all reflecting it), they would all look alike? Whereas you and I know that the light will in fact bring out, or show up, how different they are. Or again, suppose a person who knew nothing about salt. You give him a pinch to taste and he experiences a particular strong, sharp taste. You then tell him that in your country people use salt in all their cookery. Might he not reply, "In that case I suppose all your dishes taste exactly the same: because the taste of that stuff you have just given me is so strong that it will kill the taste of everything else." But you and I know that the real effect of salt is exactly the opposite. So far from killing the taste of the egg and the tripe and the cabbage, it actually brings it out. They do not show their real taste till you have added the salt.

It is something like that with Christ and us. The more we get what we now call "ourselves" out of the way and let Him take us over, the more truly ourselves we become. There is so much of Him that millions and millions of "little Christs", all different, will still be too few to express Him fully.

— C. S. Lewis, *Mere Christianity*

The more you become what you were meant to be — the vehicle through which the present Jesus is present in the world — the more "you" you become. You do not lose yourself, you find yourself.

Paul states it like this: "until Christ is formed in you" (Galatians 4:19). In other words, until the indwelling Christ has so transformed you from the inside, that your outward form expresses Him. Formed in transformation.

REFLECT

Make a very deliberate decision to be present to the presence of Christ in you. See what changes in your outlook or demeanor.

NEW WINE IN NEW WINESKINS

When Jesus moves in and makes Himself at home in us, He begins an energetic overhaul. Paul talks about "all his energy, which so powerfully works in me" (Colossians 1:29). He is making everything new so the new wine of the Spirit, who has already made the spirit new, can now flow over into the personality, filling it full.

Remember that although our spirit is perfected immediately at the moment of salvation, we still have leftover pockets of flesh that have to be cleaned out little by little. The spirit of the person has become the place where God's presence resides. "But he who unites himself with the Lord is one with him in spirit" (1 Corinthians 6:17). The person's spiritual nature has been transfigured by the presence of Jesus so that it is entirely new. Nothing old left behind. No unrighteousness in sight. But our souls or personalities still need an overhaul. Flesh and Spirit can't work together. You can't have mostly Spirit, but with a little flesh. Flesh or Spirit. One or the other.

Before Jesus came to bring new life, we might say the person was all flesh. There was nothing new in him to contrast to the old. His flesh fit just fine. But now all that has changed. Now the person is home to Jesus, and flesh is revealed as rancid and dead and decaying and it doesn't fit anymore because now the person has Life Himself in residence.

When Jesus Christ moves in, He moves all the way in. Lock, stock, and barrel. Everything He's got comes with Him. He needs lots of room. And Jesus is not passive. He does not sit quietly hoping you'll notice Him. He starts a demolition of flesh to open up space for His resurrection power. "'Is not my word like fire,' declares the LORD, 'and like a hammer that breaks a rock in pieces?'" (Jeremiah 23:29). Do you get the sense that the Word of God is aggressive? And who is the Word? Jesus Himself.

Jesus moves in and starts a war with the flesh. "For the sinful nature desires what is contrary to the Spirit, and the Spirit what is contrary to the sinful nature. They are in conflict with each other" (Galatians 5:17).

Before conversion, gossip might have been entertaining—"like choice morsels" (Proverbs 18:8)—but now it is a bitter taste. Before, a belittling comment to cut someone down to size was satisfying, but now it turns to ashes in the mouth. The rage that had been at home in you now feels like an unwelcome intruder. Before, a burning need to prove yourself drove you to succeed at all costs, but now the success it earned is an empty bag. Before, it all seemed to fit just right, but now you long to shed the flesh that holds you hostage. Before, you served your flesh willingly, but now you seem to be its slave. You have a new Master, and now you want to serve Him instead of letting your flesh call the shots.

That's how it starts—this renewal and restoration. You are awakened to the stunning realization that when you thought you were the master, you were really the slave. You were serving what you thought was serving you. Flesh has put its tentacles deep into your personality and hangs on for dear life. Even though it is dead in Christ, it will continue to act alive as long as we keep it on life support. Even after we withdraw that life support, like physical corpses, it might have a few last twitches as the systems shut down completely.

Grabbing Hold by Letting Go

The problem with the flesh is that it is familiar. We get flesh. Flesh makes sense. Until it doesn't anymore.

When we first see the process and get on board, when old familiar ways are challenged by the indwelling Jesus, who is shining a bright light where darkness used to keep things hidden, our impulse is to resist and cling to the old. Flesh likes the familiar and the known. It likes maps and charts and graphs and timelines, not open-ended calls that might lead to unfamiliar, unmarked territory.

Consider Abraham, living comfortably and prosperously in the lush, vibrant ancient city of Ur. God intrudes on his well-ordered life with a call that captures Abraham and sweeps him into its orbit. I think if he could have resisted it, he would have. His heart, once possessed by things outside him, becomes possessed by the power of the call. The command of

God to leave behind what he knew and head toward the unknown found resonance in Abraham's heart, and enticed him to something bigger than his flesh could offer.

God's commands are, in the end, promises. He commands an obedience that will clear the way for His promised provision. Notice the structure of the command and the corresponding structure of the promise. Read the command in Genesis 12:1. "The Lord had said to Abram, 'Leave your country, your people and your father's household and go to the land I will show you.'"

The command is to leave (1) your country; (2) your people; and (3) your father's household. Do you see how it starts with the remote—your country—and moves progressively to the very personal—your family? The command does not end with what Abram must leave behind. It commands him to possess and embrace what lies ahead. The command is already a promise: "Let go of what is in your hand right now so that your hand will be ready to grasp what I am about to give."

The promise is attached to the command. God is not commanding Abram to make this sacrifice for sacrifice's sake, but to make way for the promise. The call to crucifixion is always to make a way for resurrection.

Note the promise in Genesis 12:2–3.

> *"I will make you into a great nation and I will bless you; I will make your name great, and you will be a blessing. I will bless those who bless you, and whoever curses you I will curse; and all peoples on earth will be blessed through you."*

In Abram's heart, he constructed an altar. There he lay down places, people, and things that he once thought belonged to him by right. He would visit that heart's altar again before his journey was finished. The course we travel is marked by altars. We move from one altar'd moment to the next, and at each altar, we are altered.

When the indwelling Jesus begins to wean you from your flesh by revealing His surpassing worth, you will recognize that the pain of crucifixion is swallowed up in the promise of resurrection.

> *"But whatever was to my profit I now consider loss for the sake of Christ. What is more, I consider everything a loss*

compared to the surpassing greatness of knowing Christ Jesus my Lord, for whose sake I have lost all things. I consider them rubbish, that I may gain Christ and be found in him, not having a righteousness of my own that comes from the law, but that which is through faith in Christ — the righteousness that comes from God and is by faith. I want to know Christ and the power of his resurrection and the fellowship of sharing in his sufferings, becoming like him in his death, and so, somehow, to attain to the resurrection from the dead" (PHILIPPIANS 3:7–11).

When we are captured by the call "to take hold of that for which Christ Jesus took hold of me" (Philippians 3:12), we are beginning to live in an altar'd state. We are learning that altar'd flesh clears the way for the power of the indwelling Jesus to freely flow through us.

REFLECT

Where is the hammer falling on your flesh?

Are you in the messy stage of the restoration? Look at the blueprint of the brand new you: "Let us fix our eyes on Jesus, the author and perfecter of our faith" (Hebrews 12:2).

MAKING CHOICES

G od never commands us to do something for which He has not made full provision.

> *His divine power has given us everything we need for life and godliness through our knowledge of him who called us by his own glory and goodness. Through these he has given us his very great and precious promises, so that through them you may participate in the divine nature and escape the corruption in the world caused by evil desires* (2 PETER 1:3–4).

You can consider every command a promise. What He requires, He provides. If He commands, then that is the assurance that what He commands is possible through Him. Every command He gives is meant to set you free. There is a difference between following a stringent set of rules trying to live up to some elusive standard of behavior, and following the voice of the One who loves you completely and has only your good in mind.

The New Testament contains many direct commands calling us to choose obedience. Each of these commands is a call to go against the flesh's inclinations and actively embrace the Spirit's way. We don't need a command to do things that come instinctually. No one needs to command you to breathe air, for example. The fact of the command means that the indwelling Jesus is calling you to altar your flesh. But, each command has a corresponding promise of indwelling power. You choose, but your choice is to lean on the power of the present Jesus, not merely to accomplish the command.

Jim Fowler of Christ in You Ministries explains this paradox. In his description he differentiates between imperative commands—giving orders or directives—and indicative statements—stating the way things are.

> Paul's admonition to "work out your own salvation with fear and trembling" (Phil. 2:12) is an *imperative*. The *indicative* statement is, "God is at work in you both to will and to work for His good pleasure" (Phil. 2:13). Another *imperative* is, "Do not worry about anything" (Phil. 4:6). The following *indicative* is, "I can do all things through Christ who strengthens me" (Phil. 4:13). "Rejoice always, pray without ceasing, . . . abstain from every form of evil" (I Thess. 5:16,17,22) are the *imperatives*. "Faithful is He who calls you, and He will bring it to pass" (I Thess. 5:24) is the foundational *indicative*. "Love one another" (Jn. 13:34, 35) was Jesus' command. The supply for such is indicated in that "the love of God is shed abroad in our hearts by the Holy Spirit who has been given to us" (Rom. 5:5). The *imperative* is, "Be strong in the Lord" (Eph. 6:12), but the *indicative* awareness is that this is "in the strength of His might" (Eph. 6:12), for we are strong only "by the strength which God supplies" (I Pet. 4:11). "Let this mind be in you which was in Christ Jesus" (Phil. 2:5), Paul commanded the Philippians, and to the Colossians he wrote, "Set your minds on things above" (Col. 3:2), but he advised the Corinthians, "we have the mind of Christ" (I Cor. 2:16). "Discipline yourself unto godliness" (I Tim. 4:7) was the admonition to Timothy, but Peter indicates, "His divine power has granted us everything pertaining to life and godliness" (II Pet. 1:3). The *imperatives* are always based on the *indicatives* of God's grace in Christ, and are never commands for self-produced behavioral "works" of righteousness.

We have the ability to choose because we are humans made in God's image, but we have the power to choose righteousness because Jesus empowers us from the inside. Little by little, living in an altar'd state so radically recreates us that things we once had to choose become instead the heart's desire. Oswald Chambers, author of *My Utmost for His Highest,* says, "The choices of our free will become the preordinations of His almighty order."

Choosing the Cross

Each time your flesh is exposed, choose the way of the Cross. What exposes your flesh? Circumstances and people. Anything or anyone you can't control or manage. When you come across people and circumstances that engage your flesh, you are at a crucifixion moment. Altar that anger, or offence, or fear, or defensiveness, or possessiveness. Right then, before flesh starts running the show. It's there, but it's altar'd. Flesh might show up, but it won't take over. Altar it again and again until one day it doesn't show up. The altar has done its crucifixion work and you are free of that particular flesh pattern.

To have a will that operates separately from God's will is not wrong. Jesus had His own will, but He freely chose the Father's will. He lived in an altar'd state. He didn't have a will that was unrighteous because He never let an unrighteous desire take hold, but He had a human will.

> *"For I have come down from heaven not to do my will but to do the will of him who sent me"* (JOHN 6:38).

> *"Father, if you are willing, take this cup from me; yet not my will, but yours be done."* (LUKE 22:42).

If Jesus had not had a will of His own, then He would have been a robot, not a man. Because He came as the last Adam, as a fully human being, He had His own will. Like the original Adam, He was tempted as we are (Hebrews 4) to be His own source. You can see that when He made statements about how He lived His life on earth, He kept that will altar'd. He emphasized that He never acted as His own independent source.

> *"I tell you the truth, the Son can do nothing by himself; he can do only what he sees his Father doing, because whatever the Father does the Son also does"* (JOHN 5:19).

> *"I do nothing on my own but speak just what the Father has taught me"* (JOHN 8:28).

> *"For I did not speak of my own accord, but the Father who sent me commanded me what to say and how to say it. I know that his command leads to eternal life. So whatever I say is just what the Father has told me to say"* (JOHN 12:49–50).

In each of these statements He is laying claim to His Sonship and as proof of His relationship with the Father. He said, "I never act as My own source." He kept His soul or personality in its right position—servant to the Father, who lived in Him. He lived in an altar'd state. He chose the way of the Cross every day, time and again, before the day came when He chose the Cross.

And choose He did. Even at that juncture, He could have chosen to be His own source and not altar His will. The Gethsemane prayer hints at the agony of the choice, the bloody messy altaring of His own will. "Not My will."

He chose the Cross. No one forced His will.

> *"The reason my Father loves me is that I lay down my life—only to take it up again. No one takes it from me, but I lay it down of my own accord. I have authority to lay it down and authority to take it up again. This command I received from my Father"* (JOHN 10:17–18).

He knew the Crucifixion was the path to resurrection. He surrendered to the Crucifixion with His eye on the promise of the Resurrection. When we surrender our flesh to His crucifixion, we join Him in His resurrection.

> *"Or don't you know that all of us who were baptized into Christ Jesus were baptized into his death? We were therefore buried with him through baptism into death in order that, just as Christ was raised from the dead through the glory of the Father, we too may live a new life"* (ROMANS 6:3–4).

REFLECT

What choices of obedience do you need to make?

Have you been trying to be your own source of power to obey?

What would it mean for you right now to lean into the indwelling Lord Jesus?

THE HOPE OF GLORY

The goal is not simply the imitation of Christ, but the manifestation of Christ. The purpose of Christ *in us* is Christ *through us*. This involves obedience and surrender. Paul says,

> "We always carry around in our body the death of Jesus, so that the life of Jesus may also be revealed in our body. For we who are alive are always being given over to death for Jesus' sake, so that his life may be revealed in our mortal body" (2 Corinthians 4:10–11). We don't become Him. We are not "little gods," as some claim. We are the vehicles through which Christ expresses Himself in the world. He does this with our cooperation.

Jesus said, "I and the Father are one" (John 10:30). And, "the Father is in me, and I in the Father" (John 10:38). And, "it is the Father, living in me, who is doing his work" (John 14:10). Yet, He referred to the Father and Himself as distinguishable beings. He obeyed the Father; He loved the Father; He came to do the Father's will.

Jesus also said, "Anyone who has seen me has seen the Father" (John 14:9). Because the Father lived in Him, and He obeyed the Father, therefore the Father worked through Him and He was the manifestation of the Father in the world. Jesus in man form was our archetype. An archetype is the original pattern or model from which all things of the same kind are copied or on which they are based. He was the last Adam, the forerunner, the first born among many. "As the Father has sent me, I am sending you" (John 20:21).

The goal, then, is that when we live out our lives in the world, we could say, "If you've seen me, you've seen Jesus. Look! This is what Jesus looks like." He is working out a process of cleansing and restoring that is strategic, deliberate, and purposeful. The better we understand it, the more effectively we will cooperate with it. Let's look at the process from the ground up.

Falling Short

"For all have sinned and fall short of the glory of God" (Romans 3:23). Sin caused mankind to fall short of the *glory* of God. Not the expectations of God; not the standards of God; the *glory* of God. What is the glory of God? How did sin cause us to fall short of the glory?

The word *glory* is a multifaceted word. In Hebrew it is *kahvohd.*

It means "brightness or outshining."

> *"As he was praying, the appearance of his face changed, and his clothes became as bright as a flash of lightning . . . . Peter and his companions were very sleepy, but when they became fully awake, they saw his glory"* (LUKE 9:29, 32).

It means "manifested presence"—the invisible put in visible form.

> *"For the Son of Man is going to come in his Father's glory"* (MATTHEW 16:27).

> *"The Son is the radiance of God's glory and the exact representation of his being"* (HEBREWS 1:3).

> *"Then the cloud covered the Tent of Meeting, and the glory of the Lord filled the tabernacle. Moses could not enter the Tent of Meeting because the cloud had settled upon it, and the glory of the Lord filled the tabernacle"* (EXODUS 40:34–35).

Let me pull many of the layers together. Let's start with the word "outshining." If I were standing in front of you right now and you were seeing me, it would not be *me* you were seeing. You would be seeing the light rays that bounce off of me. You would be seeing my "outshining." The only way for you to know what I look like is for you to see the light rays that bounce off of me.

You can't see in the dark. In the dark, I would be invisible to you, even if I were present. So when you see my "outshining," you are seeing my "manifested presence," or my presence made visible. Even though I had been present all along, the light bouncing off of me would cause my presence to become visible. When I am revealed and my presence becomes visible, then my features emerge. My true value becomes obvious because I am on display. No longer am I covered by darkness (Psalm 97:2). Now, instead of guessing about me, you *see* me—I am revealed to you. You might say the light has made me known (John 1:18).

What does it mean that we have fallen short of the *glory* of God? To understand, we have to go all the way back to the beginning. In the creation account, the plural name for God, *Elohim*, is used. Throughout the account, the triune nature of God is emphasized. Notice the conversations that the Three-One God has with Himself. "Then God said, 'Let us make man in our image, in our likeness'" (Genesis 1:26). "And the Lord God said, 'The man has now become like one of us'" (Genesis 3:22).

The triune God is God the Father, God the Son, God the Spirit. When the Scripture refers to God, it is speaking of the Three-One. The triune God is Three acting as One; Three living and acting in such perfect harmony that they are One.

The Triune Design

I personally hold to a triune design of man. It seems to me to fit exactly into the theme of the whole counsel of God, as I will lay out in this summary. Sometimes spirit and soul are used interchangeably, but are separate often enough to give them separate consideration. Here is how I understand the triune design of God, upon which the design of man is based.

> *"Yet for us there is but one God, the Father, from whom all things came and for whom we live; and there is but one Lord, Jesus Christ, through whom all things came and through whom we live"* (1 CORINTHIANS 8:6).

> *"Since we live by the Spirit"* (GALATIANS 5:25).

Elohim created humankind in Their own image and likeness. "Then God said, 'Let *us* make man in *our* image, in *our* likeness'" (Genesis 1:26; emphasis added). The triune God created a triune being. He created the human with spirit, soul, body. "The Lord God formed the man from the dust of the ground [body] and breathed into his nostrils the breath of life [spirit], and the man became a living being [soul]" (Genesis 2:7).

Humans were designed to be the "glory" of God. They were created to operate according to the Triune Design: *from* the spirit, *through* the soul, *by* the body. I believe the spirit was to be the command-center of the soul; the soul was the command-center of the body. This mirrors from the Father, through the Son, by the Spirit. Elohim's intention in creating Adam and Eve was to point to them and say, "Do you want to know something of what I look like? Look at him. Look at her. They are My outshining. They are My manifested, visible presence". He wanted mankind to be able to say, "If you've seen Me, you've seen the Father." Mankind was intended to be the glory of God.

Humans were designed so that the body, soul, and spirit were to operate in perfect harmony. Spirit, soul, and body were to operate in such perfect harmony that they would be one. Humans were to be the glory—the outshining, the manifested presence—of Elohim. His purpose for mankind was to make Him known, to shine the spotlight on Him.

Sin Disrupted the Triune Design

The deceiver appealed to the human soul. The soul (mind, will, emotions) responded to the appeal and acted through the body. Now the harmony was disrupted. The human soul acted as its own master rather than as the vehicle through which the spirit operated. With the entrance of sin, not only did humankind come into conflict with God, but also with itself. His spirit, soul, and body were out of sync. When the one who was created to be a life container became a death container instead, nothing worked as it was designed to work. Paul describes this state of death in Romans 7.

> *"I do not understand what I do. For what I want to do I do not do, but what I hate I do. And if I do what I do not want to do, I agree that the law is good. As it is, it is no longer I myself who do it, but it is sin living in me. I know that nothing good lives*

*in me, that is, in my sinful nature. For I have the desire to do
what is good, but I cannot carry it out. For what I do is not the
good I want to do; no, the evil I do not want to do—this I keep
on doing"* (ROMANS 7:15–19).

No longer did the humans operate according to the triune original design.
Mankind sinned and so fell short of the *glory* of God.

REFLECT

*In what ways do you identify with the struggle Paul described in Romans 7:15–
19? Be specific about areas of your life.*

Can you look back and see ways that you used to struggle, but now are free?

RESTORING THE GLORY

From the beginning, God had a plan for how He would restore His glory. The plan goes like this: "Christ in you, the hope of glory" (COLOSSIANS 1:27; EMPHASIS ADDED).

T he whole Bible is pointing toward the theme: Christ in you.

"I have become its [the church's] servant by the commission God gave me to present to you the word of God in its fullness—the mystery that has been kept hidden for ages and generations, but is now disclosed to the saints. To them God has chosen to make known among the Gentiles the glorious riches of this mystery, which is Christ in you, the hope of glory" (Colossians 1:25–28).

Paul's commission is "to present the Word of God in its fullness." Until then, the message was not fully presented. It had been kept hidden. The shadows could be seen, but not the substance. It was a mystery. There was an element that had been kept hidden until the time came for it to be revealed. There was a missing piece, which, once disclosed, would cause everything else to fall into place.

But now, says Paul, that which had been hidden is revealed. It is brought out into the open and made plain. The fullness of the message can now be seen. And what is that message? What is the fullness of the Word of God? It can all be summed up in one phrase: Christ in you, the hope of glory.

Paul makes the same point in his letter to the Romans, but adds a key crucial to our understanding of the gospel.

"Now to him who is able to establish you by my gospel and the proclamation of Jesus Christ, according to the revelation of the mystery hidden for long ages past, but now revealed and made known through the prophetic writings by the command of the eternal God, so that all nations might believe and obey him—to the only wise God be glory forever through Jesus Christ! Amen" (ROMANS 16:25–27).

Paul refers to "my gospel and the proclamation of [about] Jesus Christ." This announcement about Jesus Christ had been "hidden for long ages past." Now, Paul says, this hidden mystery is "revealed and made known." We already know (from Colossians) that the mystery is "Christ in you, the hope of glory."

Where was the mystery hidden? It was hidden in the prophetic writings—the Old Testament. How is the mystery being revealed? From the prophetic writings *by the command of the eternal God*. The whole Old Testament is moving toward the reality: *Christ in you*.

The message of the Old Testament had always been "Christ in you," but only since the Spirit of Christ has come to indwell believers has the message been made plain and brought out into the open.

The Triune Dwelling Place

God painted a picture of the mystery—of His eternal plan for restoring His glory to His people—when He gave Moses instructions to build the Tabernacle. The Tabernacle was a portable worship center that the Israelites moved with them from encampment to encampment as they journeyed through the desert. *Tabernacle* means "dwelling place." The verb form of the word for *tabernacle* means "to dwell."

"Then have them make a sanctuary for me, and I will dwell [tabernacle] among them. Make this tabernacle [dwelling place] and all its furnishings exactly like the pattern I will show you. . . . See that you make them according to the pattern shown you on the mountain" (EXODUS 25:8–9, 40).

God says that in the Tabernacle, He would dwell *among* His people. The word *among* is from a root that literally means "to sever." By implication, the word means to be the center, to be inside. Do you see what He is saying? The Tabernacle would be His dwelling place "inside" His people. The tribes were to place their tents around the Tabernacle so that God's dwelling place was "inside" their encampment.

He made it clear that He was giving Moses instructions that would paint a time-bound picture of an eternal reality. He was creating a visual of the eternal reality: Christ in you, the hope of glory.

> "They serve at a sanctuary that is a copy and shadow of what is in heaven. This is why Moses was warned when he was about to build the tabernacle: 'See to it that you make everything according to the pattern shown you on the mountain'" (HEBREWS 8:5).

> "Have them make a sanctuary for me, and I will dwell [tabernacle] among them" (EXODUS 25:8).

> "The Word became flesh and made his dwelling [tabernacled] among us. We have seen his glory, the glory of the One and Only, who came from the Father, full of grace and truth" (JOHN 1:14).

> "So that Christ may dwell [tabernacle] in your hearts through faith" (EPHESIANS 3:17).

Triune Structure

The Tabernacle was a triune dwelling place. The Tabernacle was made up of the Holy of Holies, the Holy Place (sanctuary), and the Outer Courtyard.

The Holy of Holies may serve as a picture of our spirit, where God takes up residence. The Holy Place, the sanctuary, may act as a picture of our soul. The sanctuary contains, as I view it, the lampstand (mind), the bread of the presence (will), and altar of incense (emotions). The outer courtyard is a picture of our bodies.

The tabernacle is a two-layered picture. As I move from the outside toward the inside, I see a picture of *what Christ did for me*. As I move from the inside to the outside, I see a picture of *who Christ is in me*.

Many books and very fine studies have been written detailing the symbolism of the Tabernacle as it pictures what Christ did for you. Fewer emphasize the second layer: who Christ is in you.

Notice the language similarities between the account of Elohim in creation, crowned by His creation of mankind, and Moses building the Tabernacle. This may hint at the symbolic ties between the two. The account of Moses' work on the Tabernacle is an echo of Elohim's work in the creation of humans. The Tabernacle was a picture of God's purposed design for mankind.

Creation: *"Thus the heavens and the earth were completed in all their vast array"* (Genesis 2:1).
Tabernacle: *"So all the work on the tabernacle, the Tent of Meeting, was completed"* (Exodus 39:32).

Creation: *"God saw all that he had made, and it was very good"* (Genesis 1:31).
Tabernacle: *"Moses inspected the work and saw that they had done it just as the Lord had commanded"* (Exodus 39:43).

Creation: *"God had finished the work he had been doing"* (Genesis 2:2).
Tabernacle: *"And so Moses finished the work"* (Exodus 40:33).

Creation: *"And God blessed the seventh day"* (Genesis 2:3).
Tabernacle: *"So Moses blessed them"* (Exodus 39:43).

Tabernacle Shadows

OUTER COURTYARD

TABERNACLE FURNISHINGS	WHAT CHRIST DID FOR YOU	WHO CHRIST IS IN YOU
ALTAR OF SACRIFICE	"How much more, then, will the blood of Christ, who through the eternal Spirit offered himself unblemished to God, cleanse our consciences from acts that lead to death, so that we may serve the living God!" (Hebrews 9:14). "For what I received I passed on to you as of first importance: that Christ died for our sins according to the Scriptures" (1 Corinthians 15:3).	"We always carry around in our body the death of Jesus, so that the life of Jesus may also be revealed in our body" (2 Corinthians 4:10).
LAVER OF CLEANSING	"Who gave himself for us to redeem us from all wickedness and to purify for himself a people that are his very own, eager to do what is good" (Titus 2:14). "After he had provided purification for sins, he sat down at the right hand of the Majesty in heaven" (Hebrews 1:3).	"Therefore, I urge you, brothers, in view of God's mercy, to offer your bodies as living sacrifices, holy and pleasing to God—this is your spiritual act of worship" (Romans 12:1). "The blood of Jesus, his Son, purifies us from all sin" (1 John 1:7). "How much more, then, will the blood of Christ, who through the eternal Spirit offered himself unblemished to God, cleanse our consciences from acts that lead to death, so that we may serve the living God!" (Hebrews 9:14).

SANCTUARY/ SOUL

TABERNACLE FURNISHINGS	WHAT CHRIST DID FOR YOU	WHO CHRIST IS IN YOU
GOLDEN LAMPSTAND (MIND)	"While I am in the world, I am the light of the world" (John 9:5). "The people living in darkness have seen a great light; on those living in the land of the shadow of death a light has dawned" (Matthew 4:16).	"You are the light of the world . . . let your light shine before men, that they may see your good deeds and praise your Father in heaven" (Matthew 5:14, 16). "I pray also that the eyes of your heart will be enlightened in order that you may know" (Ephesians 1:18). (Light of Christ enlightens your understanding and shines through you.)
BREAD OF THE PRESENCE (WILL)	"'For the bread of God is he who comes down from heaven and gives life to the world.' . . . Then Jesus declared, 'I am the bread of life. He who comes to me will never go hungry, and he who believes in me will never be thirsty'" (John 6:33, 35).	"I am the living bread that came down out of heaven. If anyone eats of this bread he will live forever. This bread is my flesh which I will give for the life world" (John 6:51). While they were eating, Jesus took bread, gave thanks and broke it, and gave it to his disciples, saying, 'Take and eat, this is my body'" (Matthew 26:26). ("Eat"—a metaphor for the life of Christ moving to the inside of you. As His life indwells you, He begins to recreate your desires and your will.) "For it is God who works in you to will . . . his pleasure" (Philippians 2:13).

SANCTUARY/ SOUL

TABERNACLE FURNISHINGS	WHAT CHRIST DID FOR YOU	WHO CHRIST IS IN YOU
BREAD OF THE PRESENCE (WILL)		What good pleasure? "'My food,' said Jesus, 'is to do the will of him who sent me and to finish his work'" (John 4:34). (As you feast on the Bread of Life, your food is to do the will of Him who sent you.
ALTAR OF INCENSE (EMOTIONS) Incense is connected to intercession. The love that the indwelling Christ pours into your heart is poured through you as you intercede.	"Christ Jesus, who died—more than that, who was raised to life—is at the right hand of God and is also interceding for us" (Romans 8:34–35). "Therefore he is able to save completely those who come to God through him, because he always lives to intercede for them" (Hebrews 7:25).	"Because you are sons, God sent the Spirit of his Son into our hearts, the Spirit who calls out, 'Abba, Father'" (Galatians 4:6) "God has poured out his love into our hearts by the Holy Spirit, whom he has given us" (Romans 5:5). (The love that compels Him to continual intercession is poured into us; His loving intercession is expressed through our prayers.)

The picture that is emerging is clear to me. Triune God has designed Himself a Tabernacle—dwelling place. It is a triune dwelling place represented by the Tabernacle in the wilderness for which God gave detailed and explicit instructions because it was a copy of something eternal. God designed humans as triune beings to be His dwelling place on earth. The Scripture is harmonious and of a whole cloth. It fits perfectly together.

REFLECT

Deliberately offer each part of yourself to the indwelling Jesus, asking Him to flood you with Himself. Offer your body, your mind, your will, and your emotions one by one. Altar yourself.

Day 14
HOLY, HOLY, HOLY

T he third part of the triune design is the Holy of Holies, which I view as a picture of our spirit. Here we find the ark of the covenant, which is covered by the mercy seat.

> "When Christ came as high priest of the good things that are already here, he went through the greater and more perfect tabernacle that is not man-made, that is to say, not a part of this creation. He did not enter by means of the blood of goats and calves; but he entered the Most Holy Place once for all by his own blood, having obtained eternal redemption" (HEBREWS 9:11–12).

When Jesus, our precious High Priest, took His eternal, overcoming blood into the Holy of Holies, He *became* the mercy seat. The ark of the covenant and its covering mercy seat in the earth Tabernacle is a vivid picture of Christ in you.

The ark of the covenant was made of acacia wood — representing Jesus' sinless humanity. It was covered outside and lined inside with pure gold — representing Jesus' perfect divinity.

His humanity is sandwiched between the two layers of gold, which tells us that He was always God. He was in the beginning with God the Father (John 1:1–2). All things were created by Him and before Him and He is before all things (Colossians 1:17). Then, after He completed His job as the last Adam, He displayed His full divinity. He returned to the glory He had in the beginning (John 17:5). He had come from God and was returning to God the Father (John 13:3).

The ark of the covenant contained three items: the tablets of the Law, Aaron's rod that budded even though it was dead, and a golden container of manna. These three items are seen to represent the Triune God. The tablets of the Law represent the Father. Aaron's rod represents the Spirit. Aaron's rod pictures resurrection — life that comes out of death. The Spirit is the One who raised Jesus from the dead and is now living in us (Romans 8:11). The manna represents the Son (John 6:32–33).

The fullness of the Godhead was represented in the ark of the covenant. "For in Christ all the fullness of the Deity lives in bodily form" (Colossians 2:9). "For God was pleased to have all his fullness dwell in him" (Colossians 1:19).

The ark of the covenant was covered with the mercy seat. The mercy seat was made of pure gold beaten into the size and shape that would exactly cover the ark of the covenant. There is much beautiful symbolism in the details of the mercy seat, but I want to concentrate on this: on the Day of Atonement, the blood of the atonement sacrifice was sprinkled on the mercy seat. The mercy seat, like the body of Jesus on the Cross, was covered with nothing but the blood. All the other parts of the sacrifice were offered outside the Holy of Holies. Only the blood was applied to the mercy seat.

The High Priest did not speak when he went into the Holy of Holies with the blood of atonement sacrifice. The blood on the mercy seat said it all. The blood of Jesus speaks for us (Hebrews 12:24).

It was over the mercy seat, after the blood had been sprinkled, that the *Shekinah* presence of God appeared. Only at the mercy seat did heaven and earth directly meet, and that meeting was only in the blood. The priest himself did not touch the mercy seat. He dipped his finger into the blood and sprinkled the blood.

The ark of the covenant covered by the mercy seat was the one and only place that the presence of God was concentrated. Access was restricted. Only the High Priest could enter in, and he only once a year and only with blood. Earth could not touch heaven except through the blood. So strict was this prohibition that any Israelite who touched the ark of the covenant for any reason died immediately.

In Jesus, heaven and earth met. The Word became flesh. The power of heaven came into the environment of earth. God met man in the person of Jesus. When our Great High Priest went into the heavenly tabernacle with His own blood, He had become the reality that the mercy seat shadowed.

Full of Christ

"For in Christ all the fullness of the Deity lives in bodily form, and you have been given fullness in Christ" (Colossians 2:9–10). You are full of—complete with—the fullness of Christ. When He comes to make His home in you, He brings all He is and all He possesses. From inside, He imparts anything you need any time you need it, as you surrender to His indwelling presence. It's all there, because He is fully present in you. Your job is to be present to the Presence.

Jesus, during His days as a man, claimed to be the Temple (a permanent structure based on the Tabernacle). "Jesus answered them, 'Destroy this temple, and I will raise it again in three days.' . . . But the temple he had spoken of was his body" (John 2:19, 21). What made His body the Temple? The Father lived in Him. "It is the Father, living in me, who is doing his work" (John 14:10). He was the dwelling place of God. He was the glory—the outshining, the manifested presence—of God. His body was the container of life. "As the Father has life in himself, so he has given me to have life in myself" (John 5:26).

We have already seen that the fullness of the Godhead tabernacled in Jesus: "For in Christ all the fullness of the Deity lives in bodily form" (Colossians 2:9). "For God was pleased to have all his fullness dwell in him" (Colossians 1:19). Look with me for what it means to you and me that the fullness of God is in Jesus. "For God was pleased to have all his fullness dwell in him, and through him to reconcile to himself all things, whether things on earth or things in heaven, by making peace through his blood, shed on the cross" (Colossians 1:19–20).

Now earth can touch heaven! Because God tabernacled in the body of Jesus, and because the life came to earth, heaven and earth have been brought together at the mercy seat—our lovely, precious Jesus. He brings heaven into earth and earth into heaven. He stands in the gap between heaven and earth.

The life that was in His earth body, the fullness that is in Him, is being transfused into us. "For of His fullness we have all received, and grace upon grace" (John 1:16 NASB).

> *"I pray that out of his glorious riches he may strengthen you with power through his Spirit in your inner being, so that Christ may dwell in your hearts through faith. And I pray that you,*

being rooted and established in love, may have power, together with all the saints, to grasp how wide and long and high and deep is the love of Christ, and to know this love that surpasses knowledge—that you may be filled to the measure of all the fullness of God" (EPHESIANS 3:16–19).

A House of Glory

Now, you are the tabernacle. You are the dwelling place. You are the place where He displays His glory. You are the place where His glory is "at home."

> *"Don't you know that you yourselves are God's temple and that God's Spirit lives in you? If anyone destroys God's temple, God will destroy him; for God's temple is sacred, and you are that temple"* (1 CORINTHIANS 3:16–17).

> *"Do you not know that your body is a temple of the Holy Spirit, who is in you, whom you have received from God?"* (1 CORINTHIANS 6:19).

> *"For we are the temple of the living God"* (2 CORINTHIANS 6:16).

When Jesus lived as a man on earth, His body was the Temple. Now your body is the Temple. You are His house. He created you to be His dwelling place.

From the moment He takes up residence in you—when He comes to inhabit His Holy of Holies—He begins a renovation project. He begins to restore your soul. When He takes His place in you, your spirit is immediately made perfect and whole. But your soul is filled with debris. He wants to clean out all the flesh-patterns and all the sin habits. He is purifying you. His goal is not only to cleanse you of sin, but also to *fill you with Himself.*

He promises this: "'I will fill this house with glory,' says the Lord Almighty. . . . 'The glory of this present house will be greater than the glory of the former house,' says the Lord Almighty. 'And in this place I will grant peace,' declares the Lord Almighty" (Haggai 2:7, 9).

Can you imagine how breathtakingly beautiful the ancient Temple was? Yet, you—Christ in you—are even more stunning. You are a design that the Temple and the Tabernacle could only hint at. You are filled with the glory—the presence of Christ. When your soul is cleansed of flesh, then God says, "In this place I will grant peace." Do you remember the original triune design? Spirit, soul, and body were to operate in such perfect harmony that they would be one. That is the peace that Elohim is granting—peace within. Spirit, soul, and body no longer at odds.

Elohim wants to point to you and say, "If you've seen her—if you've seen him—then you've seen Me."

A House of Prayer

He says of His Tabernacle: "My house shall be called a house of prayer" (Matthew 21:13). He is making you a house of prayer. He is creating in you an environment where there is a continual interaction between heaven and earth. He is doing His work from the inside. Christ in you, the hope of glory.

You must decrease and He must increase. Let your littleness be absorbed by His greatness. Let your weakness be swept away by His strength. Let your failure, your fear, your struggles, your bitterness . . . let it all be flushed out by the powerful flow of His life in you. Take your eyes off yourself. Fix your eyes on Him. Hide yourself in Him.

REFLECT

Take time to feel the flow of His life in you, cleansing and nourishing and bringing hope and healing.

FULL SPECTRUM SALVATION

"If we confess our sins, he is faithful and just and will forgive us our sins and purify us from all unrighteousness" (1 John 1:9). When we come into agreement with Him about our helpless and wretched condition, He does two things. He (1) forgives our sins; and He (2) purifies us of all unrighteousness. Our problem is twofold, and His provision takes care of both. We have the problem of the sins we commit—the behaviors we engage in for which we are culpable and which create a separation from God. Sins that have to be atoned for. We also have the problem of the unrighteousness that causes us to commit sins. Sin and sins.

His plan for securing our salvation was not half-baked. His plan takes into account the whole problem. Suppose that Jesus took care of our sins by atoning for them Himself, but then left us in the condition that had caused the problem in the first place. He would have left us to live in defeat and failure and hopelessness. But the amazing plan for our redemption includes a remedy both for our sins and for our sin. Our atonement did not end at the Cross. He didn't defeat sin merely by dying, but by dying and then rising from the dead. The Crucifixion was the prelude to the Resurrection.

Our full spectrum salvation includes what Christ did for us, and who Christ is in us. Everything He won at the Cross, all the power of His overcoming life that was evident in His resurrection, all of who He is indwells you. He disperses His life through you and it has to be filtered through your limited personality and earthbound body, so you aren't Jesus. I say it like this: Jesus in His Jennifer form. But, everything about Jesus lives presently and powerfully in us, and the more flesh that dies off, the more fully He is manifested through us.

He is doing His powerful work from inside us. "Now to him who is able to do immeasurably more than all we ask or imagine, according to *his power* that is at work *within us*" (Ephesians 3:20). Because of His life in us, we can experience His life through us. As He makes headway in the restoration project, flesh progressively loses its hold and sins abate, and gradually disappear. We'll never be sin-free on this earth, but we will be headed in that direction. We can be more sin-free than we were yesterday, and can be more sin-free tomorrow than we are today. He has worked out a salvation that takes care of the root of unrighteousness that grows a fruit called sin.

Twofold Problem, Twofold Solution

"We were reconciled to him through the death of his Son [a completed action], [so] how much more, having been reconciled [a finished work], shall we be saved [an ongoing, continuous action that has its completion in the future] through his life" (Romans 5:10, material in parentheses added for clarification). We are reconciled through His death, but we are saved by His life. This concept is the basis for the book *The Saving Life of Christ* by Major Ian Thomas, and it has profoundly affected my understanding.

We are reconciled to the Father through the *death* of the Son, but we are saved by the *life* of the Son. Our salvation has two components: (1) what Christ did for us, and (2) who Christ is in us. We have a twofold solution for a twofold problem. Jesus poured out His life for us so He could pour out His life in us.

At the Cross, Jesus shed His physical blood that ran through His physical body. His body was torn and He died an agonizing, brutal death that He felt in all His muscles and joints and nerve endings. He experienced the full force of death in His body on the Cross. "He himself bore our sins in his body on the tree, so that we might die to sins and live for righteousness; by his wounds you have been healed" (1 Peter 2:24). When our sins got what they deserved, their sentence was carried out on Jesus' body. When His whole life had been poured out at the Cross, the price was fully paid that would reconcile us to the Father. Because of the Cross, He forgives our sins. We are reconciled by His death.

Then, that very body that had passed through the torment of sin's deserved death, rose again. He "was declared the Son of God with power by the resurrection from the dead, according to the Spirit of holiness" (Romans 1:4 NASB). The Resurrection proved Him to be the Son of God. Because He passed through death and came out alive, He had finished the work He had been sent to accomplish. He could now pour out His Holy Spirit and live inside His disciples. Peter explained on the Day of Pentecost at the Spirit's outpouring, "Exalted to the right hand of God, he has received from the Father the promised Holy Spirit and has poured out what you now see and hear" (Acts 2:33).

This filling with the Spirit of the risen Christ is so profoundly transformational that Paul describes it like this:

> "And if the Spirit of him who raised Jesus from the dead is living in you, he who raised Christ from the dead will also give life to your mortal bodies through his Spirit, who lives in you" (Romans 8:11). Stop to take it in. The very Spirit who raised Jesus from the dead lives in you.

The Lord Jesus pours out His Spirit into us—the same Spirit who put life back into His broken body. Jesus resides in us through His Spirit, and works in us and through us to bring about the completion of our salvation. He died to get you into heaven, and He lives to get heaven into you. In an ongoing, continuous, active process, you are being saved by His life.

We are reconciled by His death, but we are saved by His life. Twofold problem, twofold solution.

Two Outpourings of Blood

Jesus poured His life out once on earth, and once in the heavenly realms.

> "Since the children have flesh and blood, he too shared in their humanity so that by his death he might destroy him who holds the power of death. . . . For this reason he had to be made like his brothers in every way, in order that he might become a merciful and faithful high priest in service to God, and that he might make atonement for the sins of the people" (HEBREWS 2:14, 17).

He poured out His life at the Cross and He reconciled us by His death.

After He, the Eternal High Priest, had offered Himself as the atonement for our sins, He then entered into the tabernacle in heaven, there to offer His blood on the mercy seat.

> "When Christ came as high priest of the good things that are
> already here, he went through the greater and more perfect
> tabernacle that is not man-made, that is to say, not a part of
> this creation. He did not enter by means of the blood of goats
> and calves; but he entered the Most Holy Place once for all by
> his own blood, having obtained eternal redemption"
> (HEBREWS 9:11–12).

He poured out His life on the mercy seat.

What happened to the life He poured out in the true tabernacle? "On that day a fountain will be opened to the house of David and the inhabitants of Jerusalem, to cleanse them from *sin* and *impurity*" (Zechariah 13:1; emphasis added). We might suggest that the risen Lord's life became a flowing fountain rather than a stagnant pool. If this fountain is going to cleanse both sin and impurity, it will have to be flowing inside. It would be flowing waters—living water. And where does living water come from?

> "'If anyone is thirsty, let him come to me and drink. Whoever
> believes in me, as the Scripture has said, streams of living
> water will flow from within him.' By this he meant the Spirit,
> whom those who believed in him were later to receive"
> (JOHN 7:37–39).

REFLECT

Have you embraced your full spectrum salvation? The same way that you received atonement and forgiveness for you sins, now receive power for your life. The same Jesus who died for you lives in you.

WHO CHRIST IS IN US

At the beginning, when the first Adam fell short of God's glory, the first way that flesh made its appearance was that Adam and Eve, who had never noticed their nakedness and surely didn't even have a word for it, suddenly became obsessed with their exposure. The first thing they felt compelled to do was to cover themselves. Naked is scary. Naked feels vulnerable and unsafe. They had never experienced any of these emotions before, but now they were laid bare and humiliated and ashamed and afraid.

The first effect of flesh was to make the human guiltily self-conscious. Before, he had majored on God-consciousness. Instead of flourishing, as God had designed them to do, they began to try to disappear. They began to have feelings for which they were not created—feelings that didn't fit them. Flesh pulled them into the realm of emotions and lies and the first thing they did was try out being their own source. "I'm naked! I'll fix that. Let's see . . . what resources do I have? Ah, look! There's a leaf. I can pluck that leaf all by myself."

We weren't designed for fear or shame. It throws everything off. Decisions made from flesh-based emotions like fear are always off the mark. When flesh flowered, the humans began to live a life for which they were not suited. Never again did a man or woman born in Adam's line experience their emotions as they were designed. Emotions, which were designed to *express* the human personality, now *ruled* the human personality. From then on, instead of walking in truth, mankind began to walk in emotion. "I feel like this would make me happy. I feel like exploding in anger. I feel like I am not good enough. I feel like she meant to insult me. I feel, I feel, I feel."

We were built to be God-focused. That's the condition under which we thrive.

> "Since, then, you have been raised with Christ, set your hearts on things above, where Christ is seated at the right hand of God. Set your minds on things above, not on earthly things. For you died, and your life is now hidden with Christ in God" (COLOSSIANS 3:1–4).

Self-consciousness is not our natural state. No one except God is worthy of such concentrated attention. The proper focus of all aspects of our personality is to put God first (Matthew 6:33).

What happens when we fix our minds on ourselves? We begin to loathe ourselves. We find unnumbered flaws and uncover specks and spots and weaknesses. We can't care deeply for others because we don't have time. Every interaction with others in some way becomes a reflection of us. We're looking at them, but scrutinizing them for what they think of us.

We were not fashioned to be self-focused. It doesn't work. We break down under it. Why? Because we are not worthy of worship. The world was not created to revolve around you. You can't handle it; it's not your role. We were made to be worshippers.

I think that almost everything else that we struggle with could be traced back to the fact that we are self-focused and ruled by emotions. That is how flesh works. Through our Adam heritage, we are born wounded. We are born damaged. We are born old.

When we are born again of the Spirit, then we become new creations. Old is passed away and new has come. As we learn to live in an altar'd state, the new life in us can expand and inflate and distend and start oozing all through our personality, driving out the last vestiges of the old with the power of the new. I'm imagining it like hair mousse or shaving cream. You squirt a little out and it starts growing and taking up more space. When you give the Spirit an inch, He'll take a mile.

We altar our flesh by keeping our eyes on Jesus. "Let us fix our eyes on Jesus, the author and perfecter of our faith" (Hebrews 12:2). We don't find that altar'd state by focusing on resisting our flesh, or by straining to think and do the right thing. We can't altar by trying really hard to believe what we know is true. We win the battle by being true to who we really are — worshippers.

How many times have you heard that you will find peace if only you can make yourself believe who you are in Christ? And, indeed, the Scripture references "in Christ" many times. Yet, I could never make myself believe it, hard as I would try. Then one day I realized that is because it is keeping the emphasis on me. "I am righteous! I believe it. I am accepted. I believe it!" and that was true, except I didn't and couldn't get it to settle in. How could I quit trying to force the issue and lean in to the present Jesus?

I had an epiphany. It's not about who I am in Christ. It's about who Christ is in me. That shifted the center of gravity and it all clicked. No more working hard to believe, just being present to the Presence.

> "My soul finds rest in God alone; my salvation comes from him. He alone is my rock and my salvation; he is my fortress, I will never be shaken" (PSALM 62:1–2).

Jesus, Be Jesus in Me

I found the formulation of my prayers to be less "Jesus, do" and more "Jesus, be." That was more restful because I started learning (am still learning) to be aware of His nearness and that He could handle anything that came my way. I realized that I didn't just save up leaning in to the present Jesus for big challenges, but I could live in that position. Leaned in. Altar'd.

Live life in moments. Bring the awareness into this right-now moment. I find that when I take joy and comfort in His companionship, I am just loving Him back. He is always aware of me, always actively loving me. I am never out of His thoughts. I'm learning to respond in kind.

The more keenly aware of His presence, the more natural it is to live in an altar'd state. Every flesh-based thought interrupts my easy restful relationship and it is so obvious in contrast that I waste no time altaring it. Well, sometimes that's true. I wrote that, then felt compelled to say, it is true more often than it used to be, and it is true more and more often. It is true often enough that I see the pattern. More of Him, less of flesh. That works best. That's what fits me. Now, I'm at home on the altar, and a stranger in my flesh.

The beginning of our salvation is what Christ did for me. The fullness of our salvation is who Christ is in me. Forgiven of sins, and being purified of unrighteousness. Full spectrum salvation.

RESPOND

Do you recognize any ways that your flesh keeps you self-conscious?

Can you begin to rest in who Christ is in you?

TRANSFUSED WITH HIS ETERNAL LIFE

"Then the Jews began to argue sharply among themselves, 'How can this man give us his flesh to eat?' Jesus said to them, 'I tell you the truth, unless you eat the flesh of the Son of Man and drink his blood, you have no life in you. Whoever eats my flesh and drinks my blood has eternal life, and I will raise him up on the last day. For my flesh is real food and my blood is real drink. Whoever eats my flesh and drinks my blood remains in me, and I in him'" (JOHN 6:52–56).

Jesus shocked His listeners with these statements. "On hearing it, many of his disciples said, 'This is a hard teaching. Who can accept it?'" (John 6:60).

The words are somewhat jarring to our ears, but they were even more so to His Jewish audience. They understood Him to be speaking metaphorically. Such metaphor was a typical teaching device for Jewish rabbis. However, one of the most important injunctions in their religion was, "Don't eat the blood. The blood is the life." Here was Jesus, that outrageous teacher, saying, "Drink My blood. My blood is real drink. Unless you drink My blood, you have no life in you." This was so controversial that it was the beginning of the falling away of many of His followers. "From this time many of his disciples turned back and no longer followed him" (John 6:66).

What did Jesus want us to understand? Why did He make this unsettling statement? He is saying: "My life must be inside you." His life cannot impart life to us from outside. He must be in us. Drawing upon the best biological understanding of His times, Jesus drew a graphic word picture of how that which is outside of you can be inside of you: eating and drinking. If He were drawing the picture using twenty-first-century concepts, He might have used the picture of blood transfusion. He wants to transfuse us with His life.

M. R. DeHaan, in his book *The Chemistry of the Blood*, says the following:

> To redeem this DEAD sinner, life must be again imparted. The only remedy for death is LIFE. This life is in the blood, so a blood must be furnished which is sinless and incorruptible. Now none of Adam's race could do this. For in Adam all died. All have sinned and come short. The angels could not furnish that blood for they are spirit beings and have neither flesh nor blood. There was only one, yes ONLY ONE, who could furnish that blood: the virgin-born Son of God, with a human body, but sinless supernatural blood, inseminated by the Holy Ghost . . . death can only be banished by life. A blood transfusion must be performed and provided . . . the greatest of all transfusions is performed, when a poor sinner, dead in trespasses and in sins, is transfused by the blood of Christ the moment he believes.

Just as blood flows through your physical veins, His life flows through your spirit veins. Your physical body is a picture, a shadow, of your spirit. Just as your natural earth body is given life through blood, so your spirit has life through the life of Christ.

When He transfuses His life into us, His life banishes my death. Jesus is the life. Apart from Him, only death, or the "not life," flows through spirit veins. Remember? He who has the Son has life; he who does not have the Son has "not life."

Let me show you a picture. My brother, Roger, died of leukemia when he was 17 years old. Death was in his blood. Instead of carrying life and cleansing from cell to cell and from organ to organ, Roger's blood carried death and disease. His body had no other source for power and life.

I remember when he was first diagnosed. The very first step in his treatment was to give him a transfusion of healthy blood. A call went out through our community that Roger needed blood. The Red Cross set up a bloodmobile in our church basement and people waited in line for the opportunity to give their healthy blood to replace his diseased blood.

Through the miracle of blood transfusion, the very blood that ran through my veins could, temporarily, replace the death-carrying blood that ran through his veins. My life could be in him—just for a moment. And for that short time when my life was in him, it overcame his death. This is what Jesus does. He transfuses His life into you to replace the "not life" that flows through you.

You were born in the line of Adam. Your spirit veins should have been carrying life, but instead they were carrying death. Jesus has opened His veins and poured out His life so that He can flow through you.

In Roger's case, the blood transfusion was only a stopgap measure. His body continued to produce diseased blood. Only while the healthy blood flowed in his veins were his disease's effects slowed. Soon the "not life" filled his veins again. But Jesus' transfusion is different. It is eternal.

Body of Righteousness

Look again at Paul's word from Romans 6:6–7:

> *"For we know that our old self was crucified with him so that the body of sin might be done away with, that we should no longer be slaves to sin—because anyone who has died has been freed from sin."*

Paul says that our *body of sin,* or the *body of death* (Romans 7:24), has already been done away with. Yet you have the same body now that you had before you were given eternal life. How can Paul speak of the body of sin and the body of death as being done away with? I wrote about this briefly in my book, *He Restores My Soul:*

He says that when my old self is crucified, "the body of sin" is "done away with." What is he saying? When he uses the phrase "body of sin," he means the body (the vehicle through which we perform) that belongs to sin; the body through which the old nature acts. When I enter into the crucifixion of Jesus, I do not get a new earth-body. I look just the same as I did before. But now that same old body has been made new internally. Now it no longer contains death; now it contains life. Think of it like this: my computer is encased in an outer structure. When I look at my computer, I see its casing. That's how I recognize it as my computer. However, what really makes my computer my computer is its inner workings. If I were to take my computer to a technician and ask him take out the old computer and put in an entirely new computer, but keep the outer structure, when I take the computer home, I now have a brand new computer. It looks the same to my eyes, but it is a brand new creation. It has a new operating system; it runs new programs; it responds to different commands than before. When Christ comes to be my life, my body is no longer a body of sin. It is now a body of righteousness because the body of sin has been done away with.

Paul says that the transformation is so drastic, so radical, that his body, once a container of death, is now a container of life. The "body of death" has been done away with.

REFLECT

You no longer live in a body of sin. You commit sins sometimes, and you sometimes step over into flesh, but that is not in line with your new nature. Why, when you sin or act in flesh, does it bother you? Because it doesn't fit you. Settle in your mind and heart right now that you are a new creation in Christ if you are a Christian.

CLEAN INSIDE AND OUT

The life of Jesus, Jesus Himself, flows through me. The Scripture tells us that when we confess our sins, two things happen: (1) He forgives us our sins, and (2) He purifies us from all unrighteousness. That fountain to which Zechariah refers in Zechariah 13:1 — you looked at this on Day 15 briefly — is for cleansing from both *sin* (the sinful actions we engage in) and *impurity* (meaning the unrighteousness that causes us to sin). In Isaiah 53:5 we read, "He was pierced for our transgressions, he was crushed for our iniquities." The word for "transgressions" (*pesha*) means "rebellion or revolt" — the attitude that produces the act; the word for "iniquities" (*avon*) means "mischief, behavior, fault" — the actions of sin we commit. He died for both our rebellious attitude and the sins that it produces.

PROBLEM	Sins we commit	Unrighteousness that causes us to commit sins
SOLUTION	Reconciled by His death; what Christ did for me	Saved by His life; who Christ is in me
PROMISE	Forgive our sins	Purify us of all unrighteousness

A Flowing Fountain

"For the life of a creature is in the blood . . . the life of every creature is its blood" (Leviticus 17:11, 14). Blood is an earthly substance that God gave us to illustrate a spiritual reality. Earth blood is a copy or shadow of what the true counterpart means in heaven. Blood is the material illustration of a spiritual reality called life.

Life is in the blood. Look at the earthly picture that points us to this reality. Life really is in the blood. Everything your cells need to thrive—the minerals, vitamins, nutrients, oxygen—is delivered to them through your bloodstream. When you eat, the nutrients in your food are absorbed into your bloodstream and delivered to your cells. When you breathe in air, the oxygen is carried by your bloodstream to your cells. Your bloodstream is the delivery system for everything your body needs for life. Your body has no other source for life or power. Life is only in the blood.

Your bloodstream washes away the toxins that your cells release as they work. These are called metabolites, and they are the waste product of metabolism—the working of your body. Your cells also give off carbon dioxide, which is carried by your blood system to your lungs and expelled from your body.

The cells in your body have no other source for nourishment, oxygen, or cleansing except the bloodstream. Any cell that is deprived of blood will die. Life is in the blood. If your body were working perfectly, every organ in full health, but your blood drained out, your life would be gone. Your life is in your blood. Apart from the blood, there can be no life. As blood flows through your body, old things are passing away and all things are becoming new. As blood flows through your body, it is purifying you of all "unrightness." In an ongoing, continuous, ceaseless action, it is cleansing you of anything that will diminish your body's ability to function at its optimum. It is cleansing you and keeping you cleansed.

His life is always working in you, when you are consciously aware of it and when you are not; when you are awake and when you are asleep. The blood is always working. Andrew Murray says in his book *The Blood of the Cross:*

> We think of the shedding of the blood as an event that occurred nineteen hundred years ago on which we are to look back and, by the exercise of faith, to represent it as present and real. . . . As a result of this mistaken idea, we have no powerful experience of what the blood can do. . . . If I regard the blood, not as something which lies inactive and must be aroused to activity by my faith, but as an almighty, eternal power which is always active, then . . . I shall understand that my weakness cannot interfere with the power of

> the blood. . . . The blood will manifest its power in me, because the eternal Spirit of God always works with it and in it. . . . Just as a fountain which is supplied by or from an abundant store of water streams out day and night with a cleansing and refreshing flow, so the blessed streams of this fountain of life will flow over and through the soul that dares to expect it from his Lord.

Just as blood flows through your body, the life of the living Jesus flows through your spirit. He has not transfused you with His physical blood that He poured out on the Cross, but with His life — the life that flows in Him now, and flows from Him to you.

> Jesus Christ did not convey Himself genetically. If He had, his offspring would have been one-half Christ, one-fourth Christ, one-sixteenth Christ, on through His distant descendants of modern times when faint evidence of His bloodline would remain. Rather, He chose to convey Himself personally and nutritiously, offering to each one of us the power of His own resurrected life. No other New Testament image, . . . expresses the concept of "Christ in you" so well as does blood.
>
> — From *In His Image,* by Philip Yancey and Paul Brand

A Spiritual Tourniquet

As blood flows through my body, what happens if I tie a tourniquet around my arm? At that place, the blood is not free to flow. Eventually, toxins build up because the blood-flow is not washing them away. Little by little, the part of my arm cut off from the blood withers and dies.

Flesh is like a spiritual tourniquet. Flesh cuts off the flow of life in you. As you altar your flesh, the tourniquet is removed and the cleansing life floods the cells of your spirit. Each time you yield yourself to the cleansing life in you, you loosen a tourniquet. Little by little, the tourniquet loses its hold on you. The key is to move your emphasis from focusing entirely on your behavior and turn toward the life in you, drawing on His finished work, contained in His life transfused into you.

Stop focusing on your battle, and focus on the rest He can give you. Mentally, step away and practice leaning into Jesus. Feel the tourniquet loosen and feel life flow in.

REFLECT

How will it change your confidence in Christ to know that His life is always working in you, day and night, waking and sleeping, with our conscious awareness or without?

Day 19

LEFT BEHIND

"Forgetting what is behind and straining toward what is ahead,
I press on toward the goal to win the prize for which God has
called me heavenward in Christ Jesus" (Philippians 3:13–14).

All that I inherited from the first Adam—the Adam life with Adam's spiritual DNA—has been crucified with Christ. It is left behind. Nevertheless, I live. Yet not I, but Christ in me. The life that is in me now is Jesus Christ Himself (Galatians 2:20). He is life and He is in me.

In John 15:5, Jesus uses the earthly visual of vine and branch to illustrate this spiritual truth. I am cut off from the "not life" and grafted into the life. "I am the vine; you are the branches. If a man remains in me and I in him, he will bear much fruit; apart from me you can do nothing."

"If you remain," He says. In other words, "If the graft takes." He is using language that implies a branch that has been grafted into the vine. This means that the branch used to be part of a different vine. It started out attached to another source. I have been cut off from my old life and grafted into my new life. I used to be attached to the not-life vine, the Adam vine; now I am attached to the life vine. I have been transfused with the life of the living present Jesus and the flow of His life is overwhelming and pushing out the death that used to flow.

When the graft takes, the life in the vine becomes the life that flows through the branch. The branch has no other life except the vine's life. Whatever flows through the vine, now flows through the branch. The life in the vine and the life in the branch are one and the same. The vine's life circulates through the branch like blood circulates through my body.

I know it seems like we still have Adam life (death) active and operational. After all, that's what constitutes flesh and keeps it on life support. But I think it works like this: we still have leftover residual death circulating, but little by little it is being flushed out. As we learn to live in an altar'd state, the death sloughs away and is replaced by new, fresh life. When, instead, I let my leftover Adam life have its way and run the show, it hangs on and stays on its life support and I miss out on what the Spirit of the living present Jesus had available in that moment.

Life at Work

Let's imagine Jan, and base her on real experience. She hasn't learned that she wasn't designed to be self-consumed. She hasn't realized that she is breaking down little by little under the stress of being a self-worshipper instead of a God worshipper. Jan is a believer, and has living Jesus in residence. She truly loves Him and spends her days reading Scripture and praying and praising. In fact, she will tell you how early she got up to pray, and gush about her great love for the Father. All true. All genuine. Jan thinks of herself as extremely spiritual. But, Jan is easily and often offended. She deciphers every word, expecting to see affront. She reads insult into many innocuous interactions, and is always geared up to feel mistreated or dismissed. She feels martyred and is sure that she loses friends and finds herself lonely because she is so spiritual and others are so not.

Let's step back and look at the chaos Jan has created around her. She has driven away relationship after relationship. Those who have maintained relationship with her — her husband and children and family — all have to carefully navigate the field of land mines that is Jan's sensitivity to offense. If her husband is troubled, he has to add to that burden by worrying about how to tell Jan without setting off an incident. She can't be his comfort. Instead, she adds burden to every difficulty. Do you see where this is going? Flesh gives birth to flesh.

Now let's give Jan a wake-up call. Maybe nothing dramatic, but rather a sudden insight. The present Jesus speaks tenderly to her about how much time she spends nursing wounded feelings, and she sees that it is all out of proportion in her life. He begins to whisper to her, "You don't have to carry around that dead weight. You could become a strengthener of others instead of sapping life from them. I am calling you to a crucifixion of that flesh, because I want to give you a resurrection."

So, what does Jan do? How does she enter into the crucifixion? The next time she feels offended, instead of embracing it and nursing it, she says, "I feel like Sue meant to insult me and belittle me. That feels like the absolute truth to me and I will never be able to talk myself out of it. But I recognize that as my very strong flesh response. Even if Sue did mean to offend me, I don't have to take offense. I choose to live in an altar'd state. I surrender that feeling to crucifixion. It might stay around in my emotions and try to get my attention, but I will not act as if it is true. I will not line myself up with it. I will dismiss it and turn my concern from myself to Sue. I will choose not to take her words at face value and not look for hidden agendas. I will choose to assume that if she said something I found offensive, she likely did not mean it so. I will choose to turn my attention to God's agenda in this moment rather than my own. I will choose to let perceived slights (even if they are real) roll off me instead of feeding my flesh by mentally rehearsing them and dissecting them. I will choose crucifixion. Right now, I will deliberately focus on the flow of Christ's life in me. I will lean in to Him. I will let Jesus be Jesus in me."

Choose Life

When we act from flesh, then we produce dead works. We bear fruit for death. Dead fruit makes a great home for bacteria and fungi. It attracts organisms that feed on death. It releases its aroma. Death spreads.

Live your life in moments. You can choose in each moment: life or death. Let life flow or let death reign.

> "This day I call heaven and earth as witnesses against you that I have set before you life and death, blessings and curses. Now choose life, so that you and your children may live and that you may love the LORD your God, listen to his voice, and hold fast to him. For the LORD is your life, and he will give you many years in the land he swore to give to your fathers, Abraham, Isaac and Jacob" (DEUTERONOMY 30:19–20).

The more we just let life flow, the more the last vestiges of death get swept away and slough off. Turn your eyes to Jesus and be present to the Presence. Let your mind, which is trained to follow your flesh, start following where Jesus leads your thoughts.

RESPOND

Where have you seen your flesh operating?

Can you step back and look at the way flesh has spread out to those around you?

Ask Jesus to be Jesus in you at those moments. Ask Him now to alert you when flesh is operating in the disguise of spirituality.

SOUL AND FLESH

W hen God created humans, He created them with a soul. The soul, in my view, is the human mind, will, and emotions. In the beginning, the human soul was innocent. Neither good nor bad. Adam and Eve had a sinless version of the soul before the fall. Jesus, the last Adam, when He "became flesh," had a sinless version of the soul.

"The flesh," in general, refers to the operation of the human personality through the human body. Our flesh is sinful and unable to submit to God's law. We have a corrupted, polluted soul, carrying the sin gene.

> "The sinful mind is hostile to God. It does not submit to God's law, nor can it do so. Those controlled by the sinful nature cannot please God" (ROMANS 8:8).

Let me repeat for the sake of clarity here. When the first Adam sinned, I believe he allowed the functions of his soul (thinking, willing, and desiring) to take supremacy over the functions of his spirit (to worship and obey God; to allow God to be his supreme source). Not only did sin put mankind in conflict with God, but it also put mankind in conflict with himself. Now his spirit, soul, and body were out of sync. Rather than working in tandem, as one integrated whole—in the image of Triune God: Father, Son, and Spirit—body, soul, and spirit began to operate in opposition to each other. Paul describes the sin condition in Romans 7.

> "I do not understand what I do. For what I want to do I do not do, but what I hate I do. And if I do what I do not want to do, I agree that the law is good. . . .

> *"For I have the desire to do what is good, but I cannot carry it out. For what I do is not the good I want to do; no, the evil I do not want to do—this I keep on doing. . . .*
>
> *"So I find this law at work: When I want to do good, evil is right there with me. For in my inner being I delight in God's law; but I see another law at work in the members of my body, waging war against the law of my mind and making me a prisoner of the law of sin at work within my members"*
> (Romans 7:15–16, 18–19, 21–23).

Paul concludes this passage with these words: "Who will rescue me from this body of death?" (Romans 7:24). He has just described what it is like to live in a death container. He has just described the state of living death from which Jesus, the life, will rescue us. Adam corrupted the soul and put it in bondage to sin and death. Since the Fall, every descendant of Adam has been born with a corrupted soul. Each of us is born with a sin gene in our spiritual DNA, which makes it certain that each of us will sin.

> *"Therefore, just as sin entered the world through one man, and death through sin, and in this way death came to all men, because all sinned . . . the many died by the trespass of the one man . . . as through the disobedience of the one man the many were made sinners"* (Romans 5:12, 15, 19).

Just as Adam corrupted the soul and put it in bondage to sin and death, Jesus perfected the soul and freed it from sin and death.

> *"Who will rescue me from this body of death? Thanks be to God—through Jesus Christ our Lord!"* (Romans 7:24–25).

> *"For just as through the disobedience of the one man the many were made sinners, so also through the obedience of the one man the many will be made righteous"* (Romans 5:19).

Jesus Perfected the Soul

Jesus had flesh (a physical body and a human personality), but His flesh was sinless. It was not corrupted or polluted. Through the process of His earthly life, Jesus was moving toward the moment when He would be "the source of eternal salvation for all who obey him" (Hebrews 5:9).

Jesus progressively matured, just as all humans do. He experienced all the developmental stages. "And the child grew and became strong; he was filled with wisdom, and the grace of God was upon him" (Luke 2:40). The Greek word translated "grew" indicates a progressive growth. It is the same word used to describe the growth that started plants. It is in the imperfect tense, which indicates continuous action in the past. The phrase "was filled" allows for continuous or repeated action. Jesus went through a process of maturing. He grew, stage by stage, becoming progressively stronger. He was continuously being filled with wisdom.

At each stage, He matured in His obedience. "Although he was a son, he learned obedience from what he suffered and, once made perfect, he became the source of eternal salvation to all who obey him" (Hebrews 5:8–9).

Each new step of maturity brought with it a new level of obedience. He continued to learn by experience how to obey until He was ready to face the ultimate obedience. He became "obedient to the point of death, even death on a cross" (Philippians 2:8 NASB).

His hand-to-hand combat against sin intensified at each stage until its climax at the Cross.

At each step of the way, He was under the mastery of His spirit—the opposite of Adam's action. Remember that He was overcoming sin on our behalf. Why? He was creating in His life the antibodies against sin so that He could transfuse us with His overcoming life.

Looking again at the earthly picture—the creation of antibodies in the blood—we see the spiritual truth. Recently I watched a program that detailed how scientists in South America develop the antidotes to counteract the venom of the many deadly, poisonous snakes that live in their regions. To create the antidote, they first milk the venom from the snake. Then they inject a diluted form of that venom into a horse. Each day they inject an increased concentration of the venom until they are injecting the horse with undiluted venom. The horse's bloodstream is progressively developing antibodies against the venom. Once the horse's bloodstream has created immunity to the full-strength dose of venom, they draw that blood and use the horse's antibodies to create the antidote.

Do you see what the horse was doing? It was *becoming* the source of salvation for anyone who would be injected with its antibodies.

Dr. Paul Brand tells this story in his book *In His Image*:

Some years ago an epidemic of measles struck Vellore and one of my daughters had a severe attack. We knew she would recover, but our other infant daughter, Estelle, was dangerously vulnerable because of her age. When the pediatrician explained our need for convalescent serum, word went around Vellore that the Brands needed the "blood of an overcomer." We did not actually use those words, but we called for someone who had contracted measles and had overcome it. Serum from such a person would protect our little girl.

It was no use finding someone who had conquered chicken pox or had recovered from a broken leg. Such people, albeit healthy, could not give the specific help we needed to overcome measles. We needed someone who had experienced measles and had defeated that disease. We located such a person, withdrew some of his blood, let the cells settle out, and injected the convalescent serum. Equipped with "borrowed" antibodies, our daughter fought off the disease successfully. . . . She overcame measles not by her own resistance or vitality, but as a result of a battle that had taken place previously within someone else.

— From *In His Image*, by Paul Brand and Philip Yancey

Do you see the picture? Jesus, in His earthly body and through His man-soul, was exposed to the ever-increasing temptations of Satan. Each victory furthered the process of developing the antidote to sin — not for Him, but for us. He was doing the work *for us*. What we could not do, He did for us.

The pictures of spiritual reality that God has painted into creation are only pictures. A picture is flat and one-dimensional and falls short of representing the reality perfectly. In this analogy, the picture falls short in that Jesus never was infected with the sin disease. He was exposed to the germ, but the disease never took hold, just as the horse is not overcome with the initial injection of snake venom. It is only enough to activate the creation of the destroyers (antibodies), not enough to poison the horse. Each progressively stronger injection only creates more antigens until the horse can withstand an undiluted dose of poison, so developed are the antibodies in its blood.

When Jesus transfuses us with His life, it is His life, not just an element of His life added to ours. Here the analogy falls short again. His life replaces our life. In one real sense, I no longer live, but Christ lives in me. When you receive that eternal transfusion of His life, it has the overcoming power in it. Lean in.

REFLECT

Where do you need the Overcomer to flow more fully in your life? Talk it over with Him, and pre-altar your flesh before the situation arises.

Day 21

SIN DESTROYER

Jesus overcame the power of sin by direct exposure to its poison. The earthly picture of this spiritual truth is our body's ability to produce immunity. Our physical blood is the battleground between the immune system and invaders such as viruses or bacteria. When illness invades your body, your blood produces antibodies specifically designed to defeat that exact invader. Once your blood has built up enough antibodies against a specific disease, that disease will never have the opportunity to develop in your bloodstream. When you are exposed to that disease, it will be met with an army of destroyers already in place. You are immune. It may invade your body again, but it is defeated before it even makes an appearance. You have overcome that disease. The overcoming power is in your blood.

Immunity works by employing the blood's ability to build up antibodies against a specific invader, rendering that invader powerless in future encounters. Should the disease ever show up again, immunity is already in place. The germ has no time to procreate and invade the body before it is destroyed by the antibodies. You might say that your body is "dead" (unresponsive) to that disease.

In the spiritual realm, the disease that invades our lives is called sin. God wants to defeat sin in each individual life.

God Himself is never exposed to sin. He cannot be tempted by sin (James 1:13). In other words, the life of God cannot develop an immunity to sin because the sin disease has no access to Him and His makeup is completely immune to it. That's why He came in the form of man, in the shape of flesh. So that He could place Himself within the reach of sin, combat it head-on, and develop a spiritual immune system that could be passed on to all who would be born again and accept His life as their own. He has overcome the sin disease and longs to transfuse you with His sin-immune life.

Jesus' Spiritual Immunities

God used temptation as a training ground for His Son. Jesus had to face and overcome temptation so that He could be the victor. His life had to develop immunity to sin by exposure to the sin-germ so that He could pass along to those who obey Him eternal salvation (freedom from the evil one). The life that flows through you and me — His saving life — has already conquered sin. Andrew Murray, in his book *The Holiest of All*, puts it this way:

> As Adam never could have brought us under the power of sin and death, if he had not been our father, communicating to us his own nature, so Christ never could save us, except by taking our nature upon Him, doing in that nature all that we would need to do, had it been possible for us to deliver ourselves, and then communicating the fruit of what He effected as a nature within us to be the power of a new, an eternal life. As a divine necessity, without which there could be no salvation, as an act of infinite love and condescension, the Son of God became a partaker of flesh and blood. So alone could He be the Second Adam, the Father of a new race.

Surely He took up our infirmities and carried our sorrows. He withstood the punishing onslaught of the evil one in order to bring us peace. He fought and won the battles that would have doomed us to death so we would not have to fight them.

We can stand still and see the salvation of the Lord. Every time Jesus faced the enemy, it was for you. Every temptation Jesus endured and triumphed over was for you. Victory by victory, the antibodies against sin were being formed. Encounter by encounter, your salvation was being worked out in the life of Jesus.

Oh the Love That Drew Salvation's Plan

Every base covered. Every detail planned for. Every contingency provided for. Nothing left to chance.

Full spectrum salvation that provides a Savior for the full range of the sin problem. "Because Jesus lives forever, he has a permanent priesthood. Therefore he is able to *save completely* those who come to God through him, because he always lives to intercede for [intervene and stand on behalf of] them" (Hebrews 7:24–25; emphasis added).

The Son of God became like us so that we could become like Him. The first Adam was man made in the image of God (Genesis 1:26). The last Adam was God made in the image of man (Philippians 2:7–8). The Son came in the likeness of flesh, so we could be transformed into the likeness of the Son. Only His life in us can make us like Him.

I am always moved by Calvin Miller's depiction of Christ's condescension:

"Give me your vast infinity My son;
I'll wrap it in a bit of clay.
Then enter Terra microscopically
To love the little souls who weep away
Their lives." "I will," I said, "set Terra free."

And then I fell asleep and all awareness fled.
I felt my very being shrinking down.
My vastness ebbed away.
In dwindling dread,
All size decayed. The universe around
Drew back. I woke upon a tiny bed
Of straw in one of Terra's smaller towns.

And now the great reduction has begun:
Earthmaker and his Troubadour are one.
And here's the new redeeming melody —
The only song that can set Terra free.

"The Singer," Calvin Miller.
from the collection *A Trilogy: The Singer, The Song, The Finale*.

REFLECT

Bask in the love that paid so high a price to set you free. Soak in the reality that Jesus was willing to fight for you and take on your enemy in hand-to-hand combat because He treasures and cherishes you.

Day 22

RECKLESS LOVE

*J*esus held nothing back in securing your salvation, and holds nothing back in expressing His life in you. He could have lived for all eternity without once experiencing death's direct hit. He could have kept His distance and avoided taking all our pain and death into Himself. He loves you with reckless abandon.

Before the beginning, He had already agreed to His part in salvation's grand plan. He would go behind enemy lines, dressed in frail flesh, but armed with heaven's power. He would accomplish in Himself what His created ones could not, and then transfuse His life and His victory into them. He would do what it takes to develop the antibodies against sin and death.

What was the process the Father used to develop spiritual antibodies in Jesus? Jesus had no unrighteousness because He never let unrighteousness take root. He never once sinned because He had no unrighteousness that led Him to sin. But as a human, He had the human needs and instincts through which unrighteousness can enter. This is why He could be tempted, unlike the Father, who cannot be tempted. How did God use temptation to accomplish His purpose for Jesus?

"In bringing many sons to glory, it was fitting that God . . . should make the author of their salvation perfect through suffering" (Hebrews 2:10). God made Jesus perfect through suffering. *Perfect* means the bringing of a thing to that completeness of condition designed for it. The writer of Hebrews is not saying that Jesus used to be sinful, then became sinless. He is saying that the man Jesus, as man, grew and matured into His role as author of salvation for all who believe. God accomplished this maturing process through suffering.

"Although he was a son, he learned obedience from what he suffered and, once made perfect, he became the source of eternal salvation for all who obey him" (Hebrews 5:8). Again, Jesus *learned* obedience. He was never disobedient, but He continually progressed to deeper levels of obedience as deeper levels were required. He progressed to the point where He could be "obedient to death—even death on a cross" (Philippians 2:8). We may assume the Father did not require the same level of obedience from 12-year-old Jesus as He did from 20-year-old Jesus. Nor did He require the same level of obedience from 20-year-old Jesus as He did from 33-year-old Jesus. God trained His Son step-by-step. He trained Him in deeper levels of obedience through what He suffered.

Suffering Servant

Two times, then, we read that Jesus was matured through suffering. What kind of suffering did God use to mature Jesus? What did Jesus suffer that brought Him to that completeness of condition designed for Him? This is not referring to the suffering of the Cross. This suffering had to produce maturity before He could go to the Cross. Through suffering, He *became* the source of eternal salvation.

"Because he himself *suffered when he was tempted*, he is able to help those who are being tempted." (Hebrews 2:18; emphasis added) When did Jesus suffer? He suffered when He was tempted. What kind of suffering, then, matured Jesus? How did the enemy's battle plan become the very process by which he was defeated?

We find the description of His suffering in this passage. "Because he himself suffered when he was tempted, he is able to help those who are being tempted" (Hebrews 2:18). He suffered when He was tempted. The suffering through which the Father trained the Son in obedience: temptation. The suffering by which the last Adam completed His task: temptation. The suffering that perfected the man-soul of Jesus: temptation.

> God's visit to our planet is primarily remembered not for its display of raw power but for its example of representative suffering. A pattern emerges through the refining fire of suffering: God responds to evil not by obliterating it, but by making evil itself serve a higher good. He overcame evil by absorbing it, taking it on Himself, and, finally, by forgiving it. Jesus overcame as the One who goes before, by going right through the center of temptation, evil, and death.
>
> — From *In His Image,* by Philip Yancey and Paul Brand

Look more closely at this passage in Hebrews.

> *"During the days of Jesus' life on earth, he offered up prayers and petitions with loud cries and tears to the one who could save him from death, and he was heard because of his reverent submission. Although he was a son, he learned obedience from what he suffered and, once made perfect, he became the source of eternal salvation for all who obey him"* (Hebrews 5:7–9).

During Jesus' earthly life, He prayed with passion (*"loud cries and tears"*) to the One who could save Him from death. Does this refer to death on the Cross? I believe this sentence is talking about a habit of Jesus', not a one-time occurrence. During, or throughout, His days on earth, He repeatedly offered up prayers and petitions. This entire passage is describing the process of Jesus' training. By calling the Father "the one who could save him from death," the writer is giving us a hint about the content of these impassioned outpourings of prayer. Jesus is calling out to be saved from death—and God heard and answered Him. The Greek word for "heard" means to respond. I interpret this to mean, that Jesus asked to be saved from death and the Father saved Him from death. What kind of death? Jesus was crying out to be rescued from the sin that would bring His mission to failure and leave us in our death state. This intense suffering, struggling against sin, taught Him deep obedience and forged Him into the author of eternal salvation.

> *"Since the children have flesh and blood, he too shared in their humanity so that by his death he might destroy him who holds the power of death—that is, the devil—and free those who all their lives were held in slavery by their fear of death. For surely it is not angels he helps, but Abraham's descendants. For this reason he had to be made like his brothers in every way, in order that he might become a merciful and faithful high priest in service to God, and that he might make atonement for the sins of the people. Because he himself suffered when he was tempted, he is able to help those who are being tempted"* (Hebrews 2:14–18).

Jesus became a partaker of our nature (Hebrews 2:14) so that we could become a partaker of His nature (2 Peter 1:4). When we read that He is able to help those who are being tempted because He Himself was tempted, I think it is not simply saying that now Jesus knows how it feels to be tempted, so He can cheer us on when we are tempted. I think it is saying that Jesus overcame sin and won the victory over temptation, creating the "antibodies" in His life. He has transfused His life into our spirit veins. Therefore, when we are facing temptation, we need only yield to His life and His power running through us. The word *help* has the sense of "rescue" or "relieve." He has already overcome sin, and the antibodies are in His blood. Don't just fight harder against the temptation; instead yield more fully to His life. Turn inward where the victory runs through your soul.

> He inflicted a deadly wound on sin, gaining the victory in his own person. . . . If the Lord Jesus was to become our true Saviour one thing was most necessary — He must deliver us from ourselves. . . . And there is no other means by which this can be prepared for us, except by the Lord Jesus opening the path for us, obtaining a new life for us, and imparting it to us.
>
> — From *The Blood of the Cross*, by Andrew Murray

The One who knew no sin became sin for us. (Note that He did not become *sinful* for us.) He allowed His pure, unblemished soul to be exposed to the sin germ for our sakes. He became sin *for us* so that He could be righteousness *in us*. What a Savior!

REFLECT

Consider that you can relax into Jesus instead of struggling with all your might against temptation without knowing you can rest in Him. He walked the path before you and cleared it so that you could walk it in His victory.

Day 23

JESUS PAID IT ALL

Are you seeing the bigger picture of your salvation? Jesus paid the price for your sins so you could be reconciled to the Father. But He also paid the price for your righteousness. He overcame sin on your behalf, so He could transfuse you with overcoming life. What you could not do, He did for you—on your behalf. He paid the price; you got it for free.

> "For what the Law could not do, weak as it was through the flesh, God did: sending His own Son in the likeness of sinful flesh and as an offering for sin. He condemned sin in the flesh" (ROMANS 8:3 NASB).

What could the Law not do? The Law could not make us holy. The Law could not give us power. The Law could only show us the standard, but could not be the standard in us.

Why could the Law not do it? It's weakness was that the Law could only instruct flesh how to behave. The law came to the flesh from the outside, demanding obedience but not providing the power to obey.

What did God do? Because of the inability of the Law to accomplish God's agenda, God sent His own Son in the likeness of sinful flesh. He sent His Son clothed in the vulnerabilities of human flesh, but filled with the power of heaven. That was His perfect plan for freeing us from the power of sin—something the Law could not do. He sent His Son to defeat—condemn—sin.

Where did He condemn sin? In other words, in what arena did He condemn sin? He defeated sin in the flesh of Jesus.

God sent Jesus "in the likeness of sinful flesh." Jesus' soul had no taint of sin in it at the beginning, and He never yielded to temptation, whereby His soul would have become tainted by sin. But Paul is making a very clear statement here that Jesus had the same kind of humanity that we have. He had a soul through which sin can enter. This is why He was able to fight our battle for us.

"He condemned sin in the flesh, so that the requirement of the Law might be fulfilled *in us*" (Romans 8:3–4 NASB). He took on flesh in order to "condemn sin in the flesh"—or beat Satan on his home turf. The word *condemned* may carry the sense of dethroning or deposing. The Law was able to pass judgment on sin, but only Jesus Himself could overthrow sin's dominion.

Once He had dethroned sin in His flesh—passing through temptation and overcoming it by leaning on the life of the Father in Him—life could be transfused into us so that what the Law aimed at might be fulfilled *in us*. During his earthly life, He did for us what the Law could not do. He did it in the flesh, through a man-soul. Then He came to live His victorious, sin-immune life in us.

Jesus came to earth as a real man. He lived out His time on earth wrapped in flesh—a man-soul acting through an earth body. That was the arena in which He overcame sin. He condemned sin *in His flesh*.

Jesus' Soul Was the Servant of the Spirit

Jesus was filled and empowered by the Holy Spirit. His obedience was in keeping His man soul subjected to the indwelling Spirit. His man-soul was operating through His earthly body, but the Spirit of God was acting through Him. "It is the Father living in me doing His work" (John 14:10). I think each temptation was an effort to get Jesus to act in the power of His flesh rather than in the power of the Spirit.

Even when He offered Himself on the Cross, He was acting in the power of the Spirit. "How much more, then, will the blood of Christ, who through the eternal Spirit offered himself unblemished to God, cleanse our consciences from acts that lead to death, so that we may serve the living God!" (Hebrews 9:14).

I would assert that Satan could not have tempted Him to do evil because, being holy, evil held no allure for Him. But Satan could tempt Him to do good in the flesh—not because Jesus wanted to sin, but because He wanted to do good. To resist Satan's subtle, skillful temptations, Jesus had to be in unbroken fellowship with the Father. He had to keep His steps synchronized with the Father's heart.

Jesus, though He was God and had always been God, voluntarily laid aside His independent power as God and limited Himself. He had the body and the soul of a man. He overcame sin as a man depending upon the power of the Father living in Him. He lived in an altar'd state. The life He transfuses into us has accomplished for us everything that we could not do for ourselves. The life has already overcome sin and died to the power of the flesh. The life has brought the flesh back into its proper position, making it the servant of the Spirit.

He did it for you. He did it for me. He left His rightful place in heaven's throne room to take on our enemy on our behalf. To fight our battle for us and transfuse us with His victory. From heaven, He could not have developed the antibodies against sin and death that would protect us, because from heaven, He would never encounter temptation. Our salvation was so precious to Him that when He looked at heaven's glory and compared it to the battle that awaited Him, He chose us.

He is God's everything. It all depends on Him. Apart from Him, I can do nothing. I have nothing to offer, except His life in me.

REFLECT

Your sin has been overthrown in the fleshed-out life of Jesus. Receive the transfusion of His life and just believe that He is flowing in you and can flow through you. Only believe.

Day 24

THE CLEANSING LIFE

THE CLEANSING LIFE

" **H** e was delivered over to death for our sins and was raised to life for our justification" (Romans 4:25). Jesus dealt with not only sins, but also with the inner unrighteousness that produces sin. We are being saved every moment by his life. His life flowing through our spirit veins is flushing out flesh. Forgiveness of sins has been accomplished once for all at the Cross. Purification from unrighteousness is an ongoing process—a process that is being accomplished by the Lord Himself. His life running through our spirit veins carries away the flesh-toxins that poison us and produce symptoms in our lives: sinful behaviors. His life in us is uprooting the root that grows the fruit.

Jesus has reversed the actions of the first Adam completely. He has won what Adam lost. He has restored what Adam forfeited. He endured and triumphed in the testing the first Adam failed. He did everything necessary to provide His victory in us.

For the first Adam, the Tree of Life became a "tree of death" to him. Remember that there were two trees in the midst of the garden, one forbidden (Tree of the Knowledge of Good and Evil), one not forbidden (Tree of Life).

> *"Now the Lord God had planted a garden in the east, in Eden; and there he put the man he had formed. And the Lord God made all kinds of trees grow out of the ground—trees that were pleasing to the eye and good for food. In the middle of the garden were the tree of life and the tree of the knowledge of good and evil"* (GENESIS 2:8–9).

> *"And the Lord God commanded the man, 'You are free to eat from any tree in the garden; but you must not eat from the tree of the knowledge of good and evil, for when you eat of it you will surely die'"* (GENESIS 2:16–17).

The Tree of Life was there for them to eat from, and evidence indicates that they did partake of the Tree of Life. Sin was introduced when Adam and Eve ate from the forbidden tree. Sin brings death; sin and death are two sides of one coin. The moment sin entered the experience of mankind, death accompanied it. At the instant Adam and Eve bit into the fruit from the forbidden tree, death entered their spirits. "Not life" began to flow through their spirit veins. Their physical bodies, designed to be containers of life, became containers of death. Their problem was not simply the absence of life, but the presence of death.

The death that had entered them would be manifested in their life experience. God described for them the curse that sin and death had brought into their lives in Genesis 3:14–19. He described how death would be lived out.

After He had fully pronounced the curse and punishment, Elohim (the Three-One; Father, Son, and Spirit) said, "The man [both male and female] has now become like one of us, knowing good and evil. He must not be allowed to reach out his hand and take also from the tree of life and eat, and live forever" (Genesis 3:22).

Look carefully. This is separate from the punishment phase. God is saying that mankind might still live forever, even though death had now entered their experience. He is saying that Adam and Eve must not be allowed to eat from the Tree of Life or else they will live forever. They were already dead, yet they might live forever.

Clearly, the fruit of the Tree of Life maintained the physical body and prolonged physical life. Since mankind's body had now become a container of death, if his body lasted forever, he would be doomed to live forever in a state of death. In order to protect Adam and Eve and all of their descendants from living forever in a state of death, Elohim set a guard to keep them from prolonging their living death, or their "hell on earth."

The dilemma was this: Though he were dead (spiritually), yet shall he live (physically).

> *"And the Lord God said, 'The man has now become like one of us, knowing good and evil. He must not be allowed to reach out his had and take also from the tree of life and eat, and live forever.' So the Lord God banished him from the Garden of Eden to work the ground from which he had been taken. After he drove the man out, he placed on the east side of the Garden of Eden cherubim and a flaming sword flashing back and forth to guard the way to the tree of life"* (Genesis 3:22–24).

Do you see? The Tree of Life had become a "tree of death" to Adam and he was protected from it. The first Adam was driven from the Garden of Eden and barred from the Tree of Life as protection, not punishment.

For the last Adam, the "tree of death"—the Cross—became the Tree of Life for mankind. "He himself bore our sins in his body on the tree, so that we might die to sins and live for righteousness; by his wounds you have been healed" (1 Peter 2:24). A tree is recognized by its fruit (Genesis 1:12; Luke 6:44). What is the fruit that hung on the tree of death, the Cross? The life! The Cross became the Tree of Life.

Jesus poured out His blood so that we might die to sin—be eternally declared separated from our sins. Then, when "this body of sin has been done away with," we can live for righteousness. By His wounds, we are made whole. We now partake of His life (2 Peter 1:4)—eat from the Tree of Life. His "tree of death" became our Tree of Life. Now He reverses the dilemma that the first Adam engendered. Jesus says, "Though he were dead [physically], yet shall he live [spiritually]" (John 11:25 KJV).

While the first Adam tasted sin and brought death, the last Adam tasted death and brought life. While the first Adam was protected from the Tree of Life, the last Adam was led to the "tree of death." While the first Adam was kept from the Tree of Life, the last Adam was handed over by God (Acts 2:23) to "taste death for everyone" (Hebrews 2:9) by hanging on the tree.

The Way

In the Tabernacle, the dwelling place of God among His people, was a veil that separated the Holy of Holies from the Sanctuary as described in Exodus 26:31. This veil had a design element that was missing from the other two veils. This veil had cherubim worked into the design. Once inside the Holy of Holies, the high priest will see cherubim again as two cherubim made of gold stand on either end of the mercy seat.

What do cherubim represent? Where in the Scripture is the first mention of cherubim? You will find it in Genesis 3:24. "After he drove the man out, he placed on the east side of the Garden of Eden cherubim and a flaming sword flashing back and forth to guard the way to the tree of life." The entrance to the Holy of Holies over which the veil was hung faced the east, just as the cherubim were positioned at the east end of the Garden of Eden. The root of the Hebrew word for "eden" means "to live extravagantly or abundantly."

Follow this: The first mention of cherubim is as guards at the east end of the Garden of Abundant Life, guarding the way to the Tree of Life. They were armed with swords flashing back and forth. No one could come to the Tree of Life because there was no way available. The way was cut off.

The veil hid the Presence of God, who alone is life. No one could enter behind the veil except by the prescribed way—with blood. The veil had cherubim worked into its design. The cherubim cut off the way to the Life. Once inside, the mercy seat was guarded on each end by cherubim. It was upon the mercy seat that the blood on the Day of Atonement was sprinkled by the High Priest. He placed the blood upon the mercy seat where it was guarded by cherubim.

When Jesus died on the Cross, the Temple veil was torn in two and the barrier became an opening. He is the Way into abundant life. He walked, in effect, through the flaming swords and let the sword pierce Him so that He could be our true and living Way.

When He shed all His precious blood on the Cross, He became the Way into the peace of God. He became the Way into the household of the Father. He became the Way into the kingdom prepared for you before the foundation of the world—your Promised Land. The Tree of Life has become available once again.

REFLECT

You get to live in the Holy of Holies, the presence of the living indwelling Jesus. He opened the way for you to partake of the Tree of Life and live in abundance. Altar your flesh so that you can experience the full force of His life in you.

CAPTIVE THOUGHTS

"We demolish arguments and every pretension that sets itself up against the knowledge of God, and we take captive every thought to make it obedient to Christ" (2 CORINTHIANS 10:5).

Living in an altar'd state means that flesh is treated as dead. "In the same way, count yourselves dead to sin" (Romans 6:11). For years, those words just caused confusion for me. I would read those words and feel frustrated and more like a failure than ever. How could just "considering" it so make it so? And how could I keep considering it so when it was so obviously *not* so? I read commentaries, and parsed the language, and applied all my intellect to the problem, but could not come to a satisfying understanding. Finally, I just left it alone.

Over the years of working out Scripture in practice and in understanding, I think I have a better grasp of what Paul is saying. Though I wanted the Holy Spirit to make me understand those words, instead He taught me from many other passages and worked it out in experience until I come back to those words and they make sense.

Dead to sin. Count on it. It is a fact. I'm not supposed to make it a fact. Dead—disconnected from life. Unresponsive to any pull. I believe that Paul is talking about sin, the operating power, not sins, the actions and behaviors. I am dead to the power of sin, and the power of sin is dead to me. "May I never boast except in the cross of our Lord Jesus Christ, through which the world has been crucified to me, and I to the world" (Galatians 6:14). So, how do I count on that and act on it and bring it into my experience?

When I am being enticed into flesh's realm, and the appeal of my old man's habits is calling me, it's time for my will to stand up and choose—life or death? Instead of acting as if I am one with my old man, and as if I still desire to sin and now I have to tamp down that desire and deny it, I have to lean in. I have to altar. I have to take that thought captive and hand it over to Jesus, and draw on His life. Let Him speak truth to me: "You don't really desire that sin any more. You desire to be free from the tyranny of your flesh. Your flesh is lying to you—promising good results. But you know better. Respond to what you know, not what you feel. The flesh is dead. Treat it that way." Now, most important, let Him turn your heart toward the resurrection that will result from this crucifixion. Celebrate your freedom. Let your mind be consumed with what you're gaining, not what you are losing.

And, then, recognize how temptation can serve God's purpose. Line yourself up with what He is doing in this moment and let the enemy's schemes backfire.

The Anatomy of a Sin

Temptation is not sin. Temptation does not have to lead to sin. However, no sin comes into being without temptation. What is the process by which temptation becomes sin? "Each one is tempted when, by his own evil desire, he is dragged away and enticed. Then, after desire has conceived, it gives birth to sin" (James 1:14–15). In this passage, James is talking about temptation that is successful, or results in sin. He describes for us the process.

Strange as it may seem at first, I am convinced that James is saying, "Consider it pure joy, my brothers, whenever you face *temptations* of many kinds." Remember what a productive use God made of the temptations Jesus faced. Is it possible that He could use temptation to our advantage also?

"God is faithful; he will not let you be tempted beyond what you can bear" (1 Corinthians 10:13). Who is in charge of what temptation reaches you?

In 1 Corinthians 10:13 we find the same Greek word-root for "tempt" as is found in our passage from James. Look carefully at what the Scripture says about temptation: God will not *let you be tempted* beyond what you can bear. Do you see that God is in charge of what temptation reaches you? If God is in charge of what temptation reaches you, can temptation have any purpose but good? "All the ways of the Lord are loving and faithful for those who keep the demands of his covenant" (Psalm 25:10). "You are good, and what you do is good" (Psalm 119:68).

God allows temptation in order to isolate, identify, and uproot unrighteousness and expose flesh. Let me backtrack and clarify something. **God is not tempting you.** He is not the source of temptation. "When tempted, no one should say, 'God is tempting me.' For God cannot be tempted by evil, nor does he tempt anyone" (James 1:13). He, however, decides what temptation will be allowed to reach you.

Dragged Away by Desire

"By his own evil desire." The Greek word translated here as "evil desire" really means strong or intense desire. It does not have a specific meaning of good or bad. In fact, it is the same word Jesus used in Luke 22:15 when He said to His disciples: "I have eagerly desired to eat this Passover with you before I suffer."

Change the word *evil* to *strong*. He has not created you with an inherently wrong desire, but with an intense desire. This strong or intense desire, at its foundation, is built into you by the Creator. He has created you with a deep need for love and acceptance *so that* you will seek and find love and acceptance in Him. This need is the foundation of every desire. However, our God-created desires become misdirected when we seek to have them met outside of God.

Anything outside of God only meets the surface of the need and provides only temporary relief and must be repeated over and over again. "As when a hungry man dreams that he is eating, but he awakens, and his hunger remains; as when a thirsty man dreams that he is drinking, but he awakens faint, with his thirst unquenched" (Isaiah 29:8). We spend our resources on bread, which does not satisfy. We devour, but are still hungry; we eat, but are not filled.

When we repeatedly turn our strong and intense desire outward to the world, a pattern of behavior becomes fixed. The very need or desire that should have turned us to God has turned us away from Him. Instead of being freed from our need by having it eternally met, we become enslaved to our need by having it forever unsatisfied. We have, then, a *misdirected desire*. It has taken root in us. It becomes a *root of unrighteousness* and it grows a fruit called sin.

This misdirected desire, this root, has developed a magnetic attraction to something in the world. We'll call the object or situation in the world a "stimulus." A stimulus in the world acts as a magnet to entice you and drag you away. James is really using a fishing term here. It means "to bait" or "to set a trap." Satan has dangled bait in front of you. Your misdirected desire has taken the bait and been lured into a trap. Flesh has promised what it can't deliver.

"Respond harshly and you will feel better." "Buy one more thing you can't afford and it will bring you what you are looking for." "Eat one more thing and you will be fulfilled." "Take one more drink and your pain will go away." Lies, lies, and more lies.

The stimulus has no power of its own. What tempts one person does not tempt another. The power is not in the object or the occurrence in the world. The stimulus is neutral. Unless it is enticing, it cannot tempt. Its only power is the attraction it holds for you. *It is your own misdirected desire dragging you away.*

"After desire has conceived, it gives birth to sin" (James 1:15). The root of unrighteousness in your personality or soul, mates with the stimulus in the world. The mating results in conception, and sin is born. Sin is born of the mating between your misdirected desire and a stimulus in the world. If one or the other (misdirected desire or stimulus in the world) did not exist, no mating could occur. It is unrealistic to think that the stimuli the world offers will disappear. Jesus said that we would have trouble in the world. He prayed that we not be removed from the world, but protected from its damaging influence. The stimuli in the world will not go away. Where does the answer lie? The root of unrighteousness must be destroyed. Once the root is gone, the stimulus in the world has nothing to mate with. The stimulus loses its power and becomes a neutral object. *Once the inside is clean, the outside will be clean also.*

Temptation That Leads to Purity

Temptation can lead to sin, or temptation can lead to purity. Temptation forces choice. Every time we face temptation, we choose where to take our needs. Will we allow God to fulfill them and satisfy our eternal cravings? Or will we take the drive-through fast-food approach? Will we think long-term or quick fix? Will we choose God or will we choose Baal? Every temptation forces us deeper into the heart of the Father or anchors us more securely in the world. It's time to choose to altar ourselves.

In the same way that our fleshly impulses became flesh patterns by repeating an action over and over again, so temptation can cause us to become fixed in the way of the Spirit by persistent choice. We can choose Him over and over until He becomes our holy habit and the ways of the Spirit become our spontaneous choice.

Temptation shows us the places at which we are still responsive to sin. Temptation is a heart echogram. It pinpoints the weak places. It exposes flesh. Remember that the stimulus can only entice if a root of unrighteousness is present. Temptation exposes impurities. It unmasks our hearts so that flesh cannot lurk there undetected. It exposes flesh and forces a crucifixion moment. Temptation forces flesh into the light where it can be destroyed.

REFLECT

If God used temptation to bring His son to full maturity, can He do the same with you? And you are not fighting the battle against sin. You are simply choosing Him and His overcoming life.

LIGHT THERAPY

"But everything exposed by the light becomes visible, for it is light that makes everything visible" (EPHESIANS 5:13–14).

"The true light that gives light to every man was coming into the world" (JOHN 1:9).

Because He wants you to live in the power of His resurrection, God is working in your life strategically according to a plan that will bring your flesh out into the open and expose it. He is allowing and engineering events so that, at determined intervals, your flesh will be exposed. Why? So you can confront it, and surrender it to crucifixion.

Does it seem to you that certain situations repeatedly bring out the same reactions in you? Do you often find yourself repeating destructive behavior patterns? Do you find that numerous situations arouse in you familiar emotions like anger, fear, envy, or shame?

Your flesh has developed a pattern. The expression of how you try to be your own source and of your flesh's way of making you the center of its universe has evolved over your lifetime into a predictable pattern. Your flesh and my flesh may be very different, but they are still flesh.

When we react in the flesh, it is the tendency of our human nature to blame circumstances or to blame people around us. You may be able to pinpoint an outside cause, but that outside cause is not the ultimate source. God is always in the process of breaking the patterns established by your flesh. He allows you to be confronted with the same weaknesses over and over again. See these incidents for what they are: crucifixion moments.

At a crucifixion moment you are offered two choices: to react in the old way of your human nature or to react in the new way of the Spirit. When you choose to place blame on others, or feel martyred by circumstances beyond your control, you resuscitate your self-life. When, on the other hand, you choose to look away from the outside cause and accept the crucifying work of the Spirit, you begin, little-by-little, to let the old nature die and resurrection power emerges.

Do you see why the very arrangement of your circumstances and relationships, even those that seem to add to your problems, is the context in which crucifixion has to occur? We have to be confronted with our flesh so we can altar it. If our flesh is hidden and disguised, then it is left to work in us, producing dead fruit.

When circumstances come into your experience that engage flesh, flesh will try to talk you into rationalizing your reaction. And, indeed you might have every right to respond as you have, and the precipitating incident might have been wrong, but if you want the radical cleansing life of the present Jesus to flow, your focus has to be on what flesh is there to be engaged. Altar it. Lay it down. Let Him respond. You stay out of it.

Sometimes flesh is passive and afraid. Some flesh says, "If you confront this situation, then no one will like you any more. You will lose all value. Everyone will think badly of you." So you seethe inwardly and grow bitter, but outwardly you are always agreeable and likeable. And it works. People do like you. So the flesh holds on tighter.

God may be telling you not to respond, but that doesn't mean let the response be inside. If He is telling you to hold back response, He is saying, "Let the flesh that wants to respond and fix everything, and straighten everyone out, be altar'd. Let Me handle the situation and you let your flesh die."

Sometimes, He will call you to a response that is loving and life-giving. Your flesh might fear rejection and so resist. You might hear the living Jesus say, "Do as I tell you to do and die to your need to be liked. Let Me handle the response and don't fear the consequences."

An Altar'd State

If your flesh needs to have the last word, don't have the last word. If your flesh needs to put someone down, build them up instead. If your flesh is focused on getting what you need from someone, give them what they need instead. If your flesh needs to spend more money to own more things to feel valuable, don't spend any more money on things you don't need. You get the drift? Whatever your flesh tries to compel you to do, don't do it.

When the flesh engaged is an attitude or a thought, you can't keep that thought from coming. But you can keep from nourishing it and rehearsing it and giving it a seat at the table. You can keep it from being the driving force. You can say, "I die to that flesh."

Learn to recognize flesh when it surfaces. Flesh is a fixer. It wants to get everything arranged and positioned and manipulated so that it suits flesh. What are you trying to control right now? What are you trying to engineer? Is there a situation or a relationship in your life that you are continually managing, arranging and manipulating, trying to force it into the mold of your expectations? Is there anything in your life about which you feel compelled to mislead people? If you have answered yes to either of these questions, then you will also answer yes to this one: are you worn out? Drained? Anxious? Your soul is not created so that it runs efficiently on flesh power. Your flesh is working hard to resist its crucifixion. Let Him use your situation to do His work. Let it go. Stop trying frantically to hold it together. Altar your flesh.

Good Soil

> *"Still other seed fell on good soil, where it produced a crop—a hundred, sixty or thirty times what was sown"* (MATTHEW 13:8).

Good soil is prepared soil. It is soil that has been plowed up and is ready to receive the seed and give it a habitat in which it can flourish. Jesus compared His Word to a seed. A seed is just a seed and will remain nothing but a seed until it is placed in the proper environment. Once in the ground, the seed will metamorphose—become something altogether different. The proper environment for a seed is prepared ground. The proper environment for God's Word is a plowed-up heart.

"Break up your unplowed ground," the Father is saying to you. Do you have a tendency to smooth over the topsoil of your heart instead of plowing it up? Do you hide yourself from the Spirit's conviction by deflecting blame or rationalizing your actions? The Scripture tells us that our hearts are experts at being devious. So much so that they fool us into believing our own justifications. God describes the heart filled with flesh life, like this: "The heart is deceitful above all things and beyond cure. Who can understand it?" (Jeremiah 17:9). God wants to turn over the soil, to expose what's underneath, to get it ready to receive.

There may be circumstances in your life or people in your life that God is using to turn over the topsoil. You may feel as though the life you have worked so hard to keep smooth and presentable is being ripped up and destroyed. Maybe you've resisted the process. Maybe you keep trying to smooth it over and make it look like it used to, but to no avail. If you will surrender yourself to the Heart's Ploughman, you will see that you are being prepared to produce a harvest.

When God's Word is planted in a prepared heart, it produces a crop of wisdom, insight and understanding. The one who received the seed that fell on good soil is the person who hears the word and understands it. He produces a crop, yielding 100, 60, or 30 times what was sown (v. 23). What do you think would be the deciding factor in whether a seed brought forth a 30-fold increase or a 60-fold increase or a 100-fold increase? I think it would be the condition of the ground. Can you be satisfied with a 30-fold increase or a 60-fold increase if you know that a 100-fold increase is possible? Where does your heart need to be plowed up in order to receive the Word of God—the Word He is now speaking from inside you—and see it produce a 100-fold crop?

REFLECT

Where is the fallow ground being broken up? Where is your flesh standing in the way of what God wants to do in you?

Would you trust God's love, purposes and power enough to surrender this situation to Him and let the power of the Cross work in you? If you will, you will find rest for your soul.

PART ONE AND PART TWO

In your spiritual life there are two parts: God's giving and your receiving His gift. This is true in salvation and continues to be true as you live your new life. "Just as you received Christ Jesus as Lord, continue to live in him, rooted and built up in him" (Colossians 2:6–7). Your daily spiritual walk works by the same dynamic that brought you eternal salvation. God provides everything and you accept what He provides. God offers everything and you receive what He offers.

Everything that God requires of you, He has already provided for you. When God provided the ram as the substitute for Isaac (Genesis 22:13–14), He introduced Himself as the God Who Provides. What does He provide? He provides what He requires. He required a sacrifice and He provided the sacrifice. Remember Abraham's words, "God will provide *for Himself* a lamb" (Genesis 22:8 NASB; emphasis added). Through the Son's indwelling life, He has already made available everything necessary for living out your new life. "His divine power has given us everything we need for life and godliness through our knowledge of him who called us by his own glory and goodness" (2 Peter 1:3).

Then comes part two—your part: receiving what He provides. You must make yourself available to all that He has provided. God is very clear about what makes your life available to His power. Obedience. Your obedience opens the way for God to pour His power through you. When you obey, you receive His power in your experience.

Luke tells us a story from the life of Christ in the 17th chapter of his gospel. Jesus was on His way to Jerusalem, and as He was going into a certain village, ten lepers met Him and called out to Him for mercy. "When he saw them, he said, 'Go, show yourselves to the priests'" (Luke 17:14). Put yourself in the lepers' shoes. They didn't know how this story would unfold. All they knew was that Jesus had told them to go show themselves to the priests. "And *as they went*, they were cleansed" (Luke 17:14; emphasis added). Their obedience to the present-tense voice of Jesus released the power and provision of God. The power of God was released through their obedience.

God made a promise to Joshua. He said, "I will give you every place *where you set your foot*" (Joshua 1:3; emphasis added). As Joshua moved forward, God's power would meet him at every step. So it is with you and with me. As we move forward in response to God's voice, as we live by faith, the power of God will be released in our lives.

God is building a steadfast, undivided heart. How do we receive a steadfast heart? Jesus told a parable that tells us how we make ourselves available to what God is offering.

> *"Everyone who hears these words of mine and puts them into practice is like a wise man who built his house on the rock. The rain came down, the streams rose, and the winds blew and beat against that house; yet it did not fall, because it had its foundation on the rock. But everyone who hears these words of mine and does not put them into practice is like a foolish man who built his house on sand. The rain came down, the streams rose, and the winds blew and beat against that house, and it fell with a great crash"* (MATTHEW 7:24–27; emphasis added).

Both groups of people in this parable had exactly the same outward circumstances. The onslaughts of life's storms are inevitable. They will come. You won't have more storms and difficulties because you are a Christ follower, and you won't have fewer. Will walking in obedience guarantee you easy circumstances? No, you will have troubles. When you allow the Cross to do its work, you will find yourself in a steady place when the storms come. What does walking in obedience accomplish? You will face life's challenges in an altar'd state. "He will have no fear of bad news; his heart is steadfast, trusting in the Lord" (Psalm 112:7).

Every act of obedience to the voice of the living and present Jesus steadies the heart. As a house is built brick upon brick, so a steadfast heart is built obedience upon obedience. With each act of obedience, in big things and small things, God is creating a steadfast heart — firmly fixed in place; immovable; not subject to change.

Anchored

Once your heart has been filled with His presence, it is anchored in Him. No longer are you "like a wave of the sea, blown and tossed by the wind" (James 1:6). You are steady. You have come to rest in Him. This is His goal in freeing you of your flesh. The flesh cannot put its full trust in God because the flesh's whole way of operating is trust in self. Flesh is the natural enemy of the Spirit. Flesh is, by its nature, hostile to God and unable to submit to Him (Romans 8:6–8). Flesh cannot be rehabilitated or purified. It must be crucified. It must be cut off. The heart must be circumcised of flesh. "In him you were also circumcised, in the putting off of the sinful nature, not with a circumcision done by the hands of men but with the circumcision done by Christ" (Colossians 2:11).

In Psalm 112:7, the psalmist defines a steadfast heart as "trusting in the Lord." Trust is all or nothing. You trust or you don't trust. You are always trusting something. Every person has a focus for his or her faith. Either he trusts in his flesh, or he trusts in the Lord. Every time we choose flesh instead of crucifixion we are actively placing our trust in ourselves for that moment. The Scripture describes the difference between the two.

> "This is what the LORD says: 'Cursed is the one who trusts in man, who depends on flesh for his strength and whose heart turns away from the LORD. He will be like a bush in the wastelands; he will not see prosperity when it comes. He will dwell in the parched places of the desert, in a salt land where no one lives. But blessed is the man who trusts in the Lord, whose confidence is in him. He will be like a tree planted by the water that sends out its roots by the stream. It does not fear when heat comes; its leaves are always green. It has no worries in a year of drought and never fails to bear fruit'" (JEREMIAH 17:5–8).

The steadfast heart has settled its trust in God. A steadfast heart is a heart at rest. A steadfast heart is at home in Jesus and Jesus is at home in the steadfast heart. It is a place of quiet confidence. Steady. Sure. Safe.

Do you see that the crucifixion that God is bringing into your life has a purpose? He is emptying you of flesh in order to fill you with Himself. He is cleansing you of sin in order to make room for His glory. He is in the process of giving you a steadfast, undivided heart to replace your old, unsteady, unreliable heart. The process has some pain inherent in it, but when you recognize that the pain is a means to an end, it takes on a new meaning for you. Get the end firmly in view and focus there. I like the way Colossians 2:9 describes the goal: "For in Christ all the fullness of the Deity lives in bodily form, and you have been given fullness in Christ." In other words, Christ is full of God and you are full of Christ. Live that fullness. "I have set the LORD always before me. Because he is at my right hand, I will not be shaken. Therefore my heart is glad and my tongue rejoices; my body also will rest secure" (Psalm 16:8–9).

REFLECT

In your life, what is troubling you right now? How is it exposing flesh? Why is that good?

Day 28

PERFECT PEACE

"Y ou will keep in perfect peace him whose mind is steadfast, because he trusts in you" (Isaiah 26:3). A steadfast heart experiences uninterrupted peace. Perfect peace. Its undercurrent of peace is not interrupted when bad news comes, nor does it live with the fear that bad news will come. The steadfast heart has been set free from fear because it knows the truth. A person whose heart is steadfast knows that God is always in control; that no matter what form circumstances take, He is working everything out for His own ends. The person whose heart is steadfast trusts "him who works out everything in conformity with the purpose of his will" (Ephesians 1:11).

An active trust in the Lord is the cornerstone of a steadfast heart. It is the Lord and His perfect faithfulness, His trustworthiness, that imparts steadfastness to a heart. The trust of which the Scripture speaks is not an emotion or a doctrine, but a way of living in which every thought, every word and every act is an expression of total dependence upon the Father. The righteous live by faith. Faith is not something that you get out and dust off when things are bad; faith is not a currency you trade in for favors from God. For your spiritual life, faith is the air in your lungs, the blood in your veins; it is the active ingredient in your spiritual composition.

The model of a steadfast heart is Jesus. The model of living by faith is Jesus. The model of a mind kept in perfect peace is Jesus. What is the secret He modeled for us? To what did He attribute His steadfastness?

> *"I tell you the truth, the Son can do nothing by himself, he can do only what he sees his Father doing, because whatever the Father does the Son also does. For the Father loves the Son and shows him all he does"* (JOHN 5:19–20).

"I do nothing on my own but speak just what the Father has taught me" (John 8:28).

"Don't you believe that I am in the Father and that the Father is in me? The words I say to you are not just my own. Rather, it is the Father, living in me, who is doing his work" (John 14:10).

Jesus explained the reason for His power and His peace. In everything He said and everything He did Jesus was the vehicle for the activity of the Father who lived in Him. His heart was undivided. He willed one thing. He lived for no other reason but to do God's will.

Perhaps you're thinking, "Yes, but that was Jesus. I'm not Jesus." It's true that you and I are not Jesus. But the Scripture shows us that we are to be related to Jesus in the same way that Jesus was related to the Father; we are to interact with Jesus in the same way that Jesus interacted with the Father.

Let me paraphrase what Jesus said. "I love you the very same way the Father loves Me. Because the Father loves Me, He shows Me everything He's doing (John 5:20); because I love you, I'll show you everything I'm doing (John 15:15; 14:21). You are to obey Me the same way that I obey the Father. I obey the Father by allowing Him to do His work through Me, by being fully surrendered to the power of His Life flowing through Me (John 14:10–11). If you do obey Me the same way I obey the Father, you'll have the same kind of relationship with Me that I have with the Father—the Father is in Me and I am in the Father (John 14:10; 17:21); in the same way, I am in you (John 17:23; Galatians 2:20) and you are in Me (Ephesians 1:20; Colossians 3:3). Do you see how I live securely in My Father's love? Do you see how My heart is steadfast, trusting in Him? You will live the same way, trusting in Me."

Jesus' Relationship to the Father   Your Relationship to Jesus

Jesus' Relationship to the Father	Your Relationship to Jesus
"The Son can do nothing by himself" (John 5:19).	"Apart from me, you can do nothing" (John 15:5).
"The Father . . . shows him all he does" (John 14:21).	"I will show myself to him" (John 5:20).

Jesus' Relationship to the Father	Your Relationship to Jesus
"Everything that I learned from my Father, I have made known to you" (John 15:15).	"I am in the Father and the Father is in me" (John 14:10). "If a man remains in me and I in him" (John 15:5).
"The Son will bring glory to the Father" (John 14:13).	"Glory has come to me through them" (John 17:10).
"Just as the Father knows me and I know the Father" (John 10:15).	"I know my sheep and my sheep know me" (John 10:14).

Emptied to Be Filled

God did not engineer your salvation only for the purpose of cleansing you of sin, but also for the purpose of filling you with Himself. The work He is doing—the cleansing, the crucifying—all has one purpose. To prepare His chosen dwelling place for His presence. "'I will show the holiness of my great name. . . . Then the nations will know that I am the LORD,' declares the Sovereign LORD, 'when I show myself holy *through you* before their eyes'" (Ezekiel 36:23, emphasis added). Do you see what the Lord is saying? He will show His holiness *through you*. His holiness is being reproduced in you. You will display His holiness to the world.

Do you find it to be true that the more you know of God's truth, the more you truly desire it? The more you understand His ways, the more you long to be free of the ways of flesh? "I gain understanding from your precepts; therefore I hate every wrong path" (Psalm 119:104).

REFLECT

Are you being thrown by circumstances? Is your peace in place only when things are under control? Altar the flesh that responds to circumstances instead of resting on the indwelling present Jesus

UNDERSTANDING

"I am your servant; give me discernment that I may understand your statutes" (PSALM 119:125).

Discernment means "to separate out, to look into, distinguish between." Understanding is the goal of discernment. God wants you to understand Him, His ways, and His Word.

Through His Word, God intends to reveal Himself to us. He means for us to know what is available and what He is willing and able to put into our lives. It is not His plan to keep us in the dark, but instead He wants to bring us into His inner circle where He can tell us His secrets. Listen to Jesus say this to you right now: "I no longer call you servants, because a servant does not know his master's business. Instead, I have called you friends, for *everything* that I learned from my Father I have made known to you" (John 15:15–16, emphasis added). "We have not received the spirit of the world but the Spirit who is from God, that we may *understand* what God has freely given us" (1 Corinthians 2:12, emphasis added).

Understanding takes knowledge one step further. For example, I may know a mathematical equation such as πr^2 because I have memorized it. I may know how to say it; I may know how to write it; I may know how to use it to answer the question, "How do you find the area of a circle?" But I may still not understand it. I may know it and yet it still has no meaning to me.

A discerning heart can turn knowledge into understanding because it is the dwelling place for the Spirit of God, who understands the deep things of God (1 Corinthians 2:10). Remember that to discern means to take apart and to sift. In your spirit, you take apart the truths of God and look into their mystery. Then you put them back together into a form that your intellect can recognize and assign meaning to. You know their inner workings.

Compare this process with the way your physical brain reaches understanding from the stimuli it receives from your environment. When, for example, your brain receives visual stimuli—your eyes look at an object—signals are sent to the visual cortex, where there are layers of cells with specialized functions. Some sense colors. Some sense shapes. Some sense depth. Some are so specialized that they detect two lines that connect to form an angle and nothing else. It's as if the visual cortex consisted of billions of highly trained, exquisitely specialized observers, each of whom is responsible for one thing and one thing only, no matter the overall scene being viewed. Put all these specialized minipictures together and you have a splendidly detailed, beautifully colored picture. The incoming information is processed and refined so that all the data about the object being viewed—its size, distance, shape, color, location, relationship to the background—are assembled into one coherent image. Then this information is sent to another part of the brain (hippocampus), the memory storage area, where the new information is checked against the stored data. Then, in a matter of milliseconds, the information is transmitted to other brain areas where decisions are made as to its meaning and what, if any, action should be taken in response to it. Amazing, isn't it?

The amazing way that God created your brain is only an inadequate picture of how your spirit, transfused with the life of Jesus, turns spiritual knowledge into understanding. When you respond from Spirit, not from your flesh, to the Word of God and the truths of the spiritual realm, your spirit dissects that information, sifts it, looks into it; your spirit turns it upside down and inside out and then puts it all back together into a form that your intellect recognizes. The discerning heart has an understanding of the things of God. What happens when we understand the things of God? "Give me understanding, and I will keep your law and obey it with all my heart" (Psalm 119:34). When I understand a law, I naturally obey it. For example, I do not jump off of cliffs because I understand the law of gravity. As God gives you deep understanding, obedience becomes your natural reaction. I understand what He teaches me. "I have not departed from your laws, for you yourself have taught me. . . . I gain understanding from your precepts; therefore I hate every wrong path" (Psalm 119:102, 104).

The Goal of Understanding

God is not trying to satisfy your curiosity, or puff you up with knowledge, but to transform you from the inside out. He wants you to know Him in the deepest way possible.

Look at Paul's prayer recorded in the Book of Colossians: "So that they may have the *full riches of complete understanding*, in order that they may know the mystery of God, namely, Christ, *in whom are hidden all the treasures of wisdom and knowledge*" (Colossians 2:2–3). Once you have Christ and have come to understand God's plan—His revealed mystery of Christ in you—then you have access to all the wisdom and knowledge of God, because God's wisdom is embodied in Jesus. You've got Jesus? Then you have the Storehouse of all the desires of God. Your salvation includes everything about your new, eternal quality of life. Your salvation is not just what happens to you after your body dies.

God wants you to understand His ways. He wants you to have "the full riches of *complete understanding*" (Colossians 2:2). He has given His Spirit so that "we might *understand* what God has freely given us" (1 Corinthians 2:12). Jesus has come and "has given us *understanding* so that we might know him who is true" (1 John 5:20). He wants to "*fill you with the knowledge of his will through all spiritual wisdom and understanding*" (Colossians 1:9). We live in the fullness of God's grace, which He "lavished on us with *all wisdom and understanding*" (Ephesians 1:8). He wants us to have "a *full understanding* of every good thing we have in Christ" (Philemon 6) (emphases added).

Why? Because if we know what could be ours in Christ, we won't settle for anything less. If we recognize what God is doing, we will cooperate with the process. If we have discernment, we will see how one part fits with the other, and how one action leads to an outcome. We won't go through life like babies, stamping our feet and demanding our way. We will be working in concert with the indwelling Jesus to hasten the time when "we all reach unity in the faith and in the knowledge of the Son of God and *become mature*, attaining to the *whole measure of the fullness of Christ*" (Ephesians 4:13; emphasis added).

Baby Flesh

A baby in the womb has a very small world and he is the only person in it. When that baby is born, the perimeters of his world greatly expand, but the center of his world stays fixed. He can only interpret anything outside himself by how it relates to him. As far as he knows, every person who exists has but one purpose: to make his world conform to his desires. It's just adorable. It creates in us an enormous love and drive to meet his needs. We don't consider it an imposition. That's just how it is supposed to be.

But 16 years later, if the person still has that world view, then he has created heartache and chaos for himself and everyone who loves him. Maturity is essential. Maturing is a process, and we have to be on board for its momentum. Maturity brings with it its own reward. When we mature in Christ, we have more access to all of Him—the whole measure of the fullness of Christ. Not because now He is more accessible, but because we are. He never changes. He is always right there, at the ready, longing to give and pour out into our lives. But the baby ways of our flesh block the flow and refuse the gift. Babies only know the surface of things. The indwelling Jesus wants to reveal the depths. Altar your flesh and let all the treasures of wisdom and knowledge flow from Him.

REFLECT

At what point are you finding it difficult to obey what you know God is telling you? Do you believe that it is because, at a deep level, you do not understand it? Would you ask God to give you discernment so that you can understand?

Day 30

I WANT MORE

The ability to discern truth is a result of the active and present work of the Spirit in your mind and understanding. He creates a discerning heart as He lives in you and has more and more access to you. It is Jesus' own discernment being given to you that brings understanding. The Spirit and He alone knows the heart and mind of the Father and the Son. He is teaching you, guiding you into truth. When He teaches you, knowledge becomes understanding and you have a discerning heart.

> "But when he, the Spirit of truth, comes, he will guide you into all truth. He will not speak on his own; he will speak only what he hears, and he will tell you what is yet to come. He will bring glory to me by taking from what is mine and making it known to you. All that belongs to the Father is mine. That is why I said the Spirit will take from what is mine and make it known to you" (JOHN 16:13–15).

The cry of a discerning heart is, "Show me your ways, O Lord; teach me your paths" (Psalm 25:4). *Show* me your ways.

Cooking is not a skill that comes naturally to me. However, I have a friend for whom putting together a wonderful meal seems effortless. From time to time, I call on her expertise. "Libby, tell me how you make that delicious casserole," I say. Libby begins to describe exactly how to make the casserole, but she is using words like *mince, sauté,* and other terms that are outside my vocabulary. Finally she says, "Come over. I'll *show* you how to make it." Now she enters right into my experience and shows me what to do. Then I understand.

Show me your ways, O Lord! He is not teaching you on an academic, arm's-length plain. He is entering into your now. He is engaging with you in the first person. He is fully investing Himself in your experience and He is causing you to understand. When you understand any spiritual truth, it is because the process of discernment has occurred in your spirit. When that truth begins to transform your life—your actions and your thought processes—then discernment has created understanding. "Who is wise? He will realize these things. Who is discerning? He will understand them. The ways of the Lord are right. The righteous walk in them, but the rebellious stumble in them" (Hosea 14:9).

You know the saying, "The more I know the more I know I don't know." As the living present indwelling Jesus moves you into the depths of the kingdom and shows you the riches stored in secret places, the more you crave Him. You know the supply of understanding and truth is inexhaustible. The riches of the kingdom are never used up, just used in and for. They grow and multiply with use. You never have to conserve the kingdom's resources. You can be greedy when it comes to the things that Jesus wants to show you. Your waking prayer becomes, "More!"

My niece Amy, when she was a little girl, was staying with my parents. My mother was pouring syrup on her pancakes one morning. When Mom stopped pouring, Amy said, "Put some more." My mother responded, "Oh, I think that's enough." Amy said, "But I don't like enough. I like too much!" When it comes to the things of the Spirit of God, I'm just like Amy. I want too much. I want to superabound. And I can trust God with that desire because He is able to make me overflow and slosh over with His abundance.

Sloshing Over

He wants to live in you to live through you. He wants what flows from your life into the lives of others to be Him, not your flesh. To that end, He fills you up so completely that He sloshes over. What spills out of you spontaneously is not the old flesh habits, but the fullness of Jesus. "And God is able to make *all* grace abound to you, so that in *all* things at *all* times, having *all* that you need, you will *abound* in *every* good work" (2 Corinthians 9:8, emphasis added). The Greek word translated "abound" is *perisseuo* and it means "to superabound; to have excess; to have more than enough."

This inward change that is finding outward expression is so drastic that it even begins to transform your words. Our words are the hardest things to get under control. Even when we mean well our words often get in the way. To give the indwelling Jesus so much room to maneuver — flesh out of the way — that He can even transform our words is miraculous, but possible. "Wisdom is found on the lips of the discerning" (Proverbs 10:13).

Once you have a discerning heart so that your mind is filled with understanding of the deep truths of God, then that understanding begins to flow from your mouth as water flows from a fountain. "The mouth of the wise is a fountain of life. . . . The mouth of the righteous flows with wisdom" (Proverbs 10:11, 31). The heart is the wellspring of life — the source from which all else flows (Proverbs 4:23). What flows out of a discerning heart are words of life.

Talk the Talk

Jesus said that words are how the inner being is revealed. "The good man brings good things out of the good stored up in his heart, and the evil man brings evil things out of the evil stored up in his heart. For out of the overflow of his heart his mouth speaks" (Luke 6:45). If your heart, or mind, is filled with the fruit of discernment — understanding generated by the Spirit — then you begin to speak things taught by the Spirit. These words, because they were originated in the Spirit, are spiritual words and they convey spiritual truth and carry spiritual power (1 Corinthians 2:13; John 3:6). Jesus said of His own words, "The Spirit gives life; the flesh counts for nothing. The words I have spoken to you are spirit and they are life" (John 6:63). Only He has the words that are life (John 6:68). Jesus' words were spirit and life because the Spirit had given life to them — had breathed into them the breath of life. Words that come from the flesh do not have life or power in them. They count for nothing. The discerning heart is filled with the life of Christ and from that Christ-filled repository spills forth His words — words that are spirit and life.

The person with a discerning heart will find himself speaking words that are uplifting, instructive, encouraging, life-giving. The person with a discerning heart knows "the word that sustains the weary" (Isaiah 50:4). He will not have to struggle and strive to come up with these life-filled words; they will be the natural fruit of his discerning heart. "A wise man's heart guides his mouth, and his lips promote instruction" (Proverbs 16:23).

Words, words, words. The Scripture is full of teaching about the power of words. God's words created the universe, and our words have life and death in them. Remember how we are understanding life and death. Life flows from Jesus, death flows from flesh. Jesus told a parable about words, and here is how it is recorded in Luke:

> "No good tree bears bad fruit, nor does a bad tree bear good fruit. Each tree is recognized by its own fruit. People do not pick figs from thornbushes, or grapes from briers. The good man brings good things out of the good stored up in his heart, and the evil man brings evil things out of the evil stored up in his heart. For out of the overflow of his heart his mouth speaks" (Luke 6:43–45).

Words are perhaps the best measure of what fills our hearts. Jesus fill us so full that even our words are transformed. Learn to lean in when words are needed. Learn to speak only from an altar'd state. You can say nice, kind, compassionate words from your flesh, but you can't say words that are Spirit and life.

REFLECT

Ask the living indwelling present Jesus to be the source of all your words.

Day 31
SEEK THE KINGDOM

$\mathcal{G}$ ive your imagination free reign for a moment. Put yourself into this picture. See it and feel it and hear it and smell it.

You've been walking for hours and hours and hours. The heat is excruciating. The terrain you're hiking is hostile: uneven, rocky, uphill. Your feet are killing you. They are aching and burning and so swollen you're sure you'll have to cut your shoes off to get your feet out of them. You can't think of anything except your miserable, throbbing, burning feet! If only you could find relief for your feet!

Listen! Rushing water? Could it be? Is there a river just ahead? Hope turns to anticipation as you run toward the sound and glimpse a river. Cool, fresh, sparkling water rushing in torrents through the landscape. Inviting you. Offering refreshment and relief. You know that all you have to do is immerse your feet in the river water.

Sit down by the water's edge. As you eagerly peel your shoes and your socks from your tortured feet, already you can feel the water's spray touching you with the offer of renewal. Feel the water as it wraps your feet—your hot, tired, swollen feet—in relief. Ahh! Sit still and let the healing waters do their work.

The agony in your feet subsides and now you can think beyond your immediate need. The river beckons. Immerse more of your hot, tired body in its cooling, cleansing flow. Wade out until you are knee-deep.

The water courses around you and you become more aware of its power. Wade deeper. Walk out until the water is waist-high. Not only do you experience the reenergizing effects of the river, but the deeper you go, the more of its power and strength you encounter. Now you have to work harder to walk through the water. The river has a path and an agenda of its own and it pulls at you. Hardest of all is to stand still in the mighty, rushing waters.

Deeper still. The water is over your head. Now you have only one option: give yourself to the river's flow. No longer can you move in the river; now the river moves you. Surrender.

The River That Flows from the Presence of God

The prophet Ezekiel had a vision. In his vision, a man showed him a river flowing from the Temple. Read about Ezekiel's experience with the river that flowed from the presence of God, the Temple:

> *"As the man went eastward with a measuring line in his hand, he measured off a thousand cubits and then led me through water that was ankle-deep. He measured off another thousand cubits and led me through water that was knee-deep. He measured off another thousand and led me through water that was up to the waist. He measured off another thousand, but now it was a river that I could not cross, because the water had risen and was deep enough to swim, in a river that no one could cross"* (Ezekiel 47:3–5).

Water is nearly always a symbol of the Spirit of God. Ezekiel learned that you can wade on the fringes where the water is ankle-deep, or you can plunge into the depths. Where would you like to be? Have you had enough of skirting the edges of the kingdom of God? Are you feeling His tug? Do you sense Him calling you to the deep places? Is there something in you that tells you there's more? Are you thirsty—longing for a fullness you've not yet experienced?

As you commit yourself to seeking the fullness of the kingdom, let the Spirit Himself—the River of God—do the work. Your job? Surrender! Keep drawing your life from Him. Jeremiah calls Him "the Lord, the spring of living water" (Jeremiah 17:13). Don't look anywhere else for your hope, or your strength, or your healing. Look to Him. Live in an altar'd state.

Twofold Revelation

The life of Jesus coursing through you like a river changes the landscape of your soul. He changes your perspective and your perceptions and recreates your desires and your responses. This absolute and unqualified change is based on a twofold revelation: the revelation of who God is and the revelation of who I am.

Remember Isaiah? He saw the Lord, high and exalted. He saw the glory and the holiness. Instinctively he cried out: "Woe to me! . . . I am ruined! For I am a man of unclean lips, and I live among a people of unclean lips, and my eyes have seen the King, the Lord Almighty" (Isaiah 5:3–6).

And Job? "'My ears had heard of you but now my eyes have seen you. Therefore I despise myself and repent in dust and ashes'" (Job 42:5–6).

His holiness exposes your sinfulness. His strength reveals your weakness. His faithfulness lays bare your faithlessness. Only in the light of His presence can we see the truth about ourselves. "In your light we see light" (Psalm 36:9). "Everything exposed by the light becomes visible, for it is light that makes everything visible" (Ephesians 5:13–14).

Until you have a true picture of yourself, you will be unable to enter into the depths of the kingdom. The stark contrast between the Holy One in His splendor and me in my filthy rags—the revelation of His worthiness and my unworthiness—compels me to fall on my face in awe. You see, the awe comes not only from His majesty, but from the fact that He seeks *me* out; that He delights in *me*; that He loves *my* presence. Me! In all my weakness. In all my failure. In all my sin. His blood-stained love reaches out and draws me into His presence. Brings His presence so near that He resides in me.

As you come face-to-face with your own weakness and your own sin, you have two possible paths. You can either respond to your enemy's condemnation, or you can respond to the Spirit's conviction.

You have a wily, crafty, scheming enemy named Satan. One of his most successful ploys is to accuse you and condemn you. In fact, in the kingdom, he has earned the nickname, "the accuser" (Revelation 12:10). His purpose is to discourage you and to convince you that you do not belong in the Lord's presence. He hopes to use your failure to drive a wedge between you and Jesus. He intends for the revelation of your unworthiness to shame you into avoiding the Holy One.

The Spirit of God, though, has a different purpose for revealing your unworthiness. His intent is to drive you into Jesus' open arms where you will find cleansing, healing, forgiveness. His objective is that the force of Jesus' love will be all the more evident as you recognize that it is undeserved, unearned, unmerited—and yet He has settled His love on you. It is immoveable. It will not let you go.

"'Though the mountains be shaken and the hills be removed, yet my unfailing love for you will not be shaken nor my covenant of peace be removed,' says the Lord, who has compassion on you" (ISAIAH 54:10).

As you see clearly both who He is and who you are, the focus and the reason for your joy and confidence is *who He is*. The foundation of this relationship is His faithfulness. It all rests on His constancy, His unwavering commitment to you. "If we are faithless, he will remain faithful, for he cannot disown himself" (2 Timothy 2:13).

You may sometimes have the feeling that God is disappointed in you. "How could He not be disappointed?" you reason. "I let Him down again and again. I promise, and then I fail."

I don't believe God is ever disappointed in you. What does it mean to disappoint someone? It means that you have failed to meet that person's expectations. For you to disappoint God, He would have to think you were going to behave one way, then be surprised when you behave another way. God knows you better than you know yourself. "He knows how we are formed, he remembers that we are dust" (Psalm 103:14).

You are disappointed in yourself when you fall, but God is not disappointed in you. Every time we fall short of our own expectations, it is a reminder that "apart from [Him] you can do nothing" (John 15:5). It does not surprise Him when you fall. It's part of the training process by which He is teaching you that you cannot trust in your own flesh. He is proving to you the frailty of your best efforts. He is allowing your failures to drive you to His heart.

Your weakness opens the door to His power. "Therefore I will boast all the more gladly about my weaknesses, so that Christ's power may rest on me. . . . For when I am weak, then I am strong" (2 Corinthians 12:10).

You may sway in the wind and the rain, but He does not. He remains unchanged.

"O Lord God Almighty, who is like you? You are mighty, O Lord, and your faithfulness surrounds you" (PSALM 89:8).

Lessons of Weakness

How can you take the lessons learned in the weakness of your flesh and let them bring power in the Spirit? Learn to acknowledge that every single time you act in your flesh, you will fall short. Each time you find yourself in a moment of failure because your flesh promised what it couldn't deliver, let it reinforce the truth. Then, altar it and let it go. Your enemy will want to revisit it and review it, but don't go there with him. When you learn to live in an altar'd state, failures and fallings are left on the altar.

REFLECT

Altar your failures and guilt. Don't carry them around any more. Wade into the River and dive deep.

A CONSUMING FIRE

The Scripture gives yet another description of the presence of God. Fire.

The power of a fierce, raging, white-hot fire is awesome. Everything in its path is consumed by it. No power can control it. It sends out scorching heat and smoke and ash for hundreds of miles beyond itself. Trained firefighters with chemicals and machines of all sorts are helpless before it. Nothing it touches is left the same.

"The Lord your God is a consuming fire" (Deuteronomy 4:24). Over and over again, Almighty God appeared to the eyes of human beings in the form of fire. He led the Israelites through the desert in a pillar of fire by night. He appeared to Moses in the burning bush. His presence on Mt. Sinai covered the mountain with smoke because He had descended on it as fire. "To the Israelites the glory of the Lord looked like a consuming fire on top of the mountain" (Exodus 24:17). His presence hovered over the Tabernacle in the desert as fire. "On the day the tabernacle, the Tent of the Testimony, was set up, the cloud covered it. From evening till morning the cloud above the tabernacle looked like fire" (Numbers 9:15). God is a consuming fire. You cannot experience His presence and stay the same.

The Tabernacle that God commanded the Israelites to build was a detailed picture of Christ. Everything about it, from the materials that were used to its size and dimensions, foreshadowed Jesus. God gave Moses explicit, exact instructions for every detail. God reminded Moses to make everything exactly like the pattern He had given. This was because the Tabernacle was a copy of what is in heaven (Hebrews 8:5). The Israelites followed the instructions precisely. When the Tabernacle was completed, the people had a place and a pattern for worship.

When the worshipper entered the outer courtyard of the Tabernacle, he encountered the altar of sacrifice. The worshipper could go no deeper into the Tabernacle until he had presented a sacrifice for his sins. He was required to offer the best from his own livestock. He shed its blood—gave it up completely—and laid it on the altar.

At the Tabernacle's dedication, the people brought their sacrifices and placed them on the altar. The Scripture records what happened next: "Fire came out from the presence of the Lord and consumed the burnt offering and the fat portions on the altar. And when all the people saw it, they shouted for joy and fell facedown" (Leviticus 9:24).

When God accepted and consumed their sacrifices, the power of His presence caused the people to worship. Worship is the soul's spontaneous response to the presence of God.

For you, the altar is the Cross of Jesus. At the Cross, He offered Himself to be the sacrifice for you. Now He calls you to offer yourself as a living sacrifice. Surrender all that you are, all that you have been, all that you will be. Give it up completely. Altar it. Your act of altaring your flesh is an act of worship that acknowledges who God is. Every time you choose to lean in to Jesus instead of acting in flesh, you are worshipping. You are acknowledging that God is able, and faithful, and trustworthy.

Cleansing Fire

The fire of His presence is not a destroying fire, but a cleansing fire. It will burn away all the earth stuff that clings to you and holds you back from venturing deep into the kingdom.

The Messiah is like a refiner's fire. He will sit as a refiner and purifier of silver (Malachi 3:2–3). Silver is refined by heat. The heat melts the silver and then causes the impurities to rise to the top so they can be skimmed off. The word *pure* means "unmixed, unalloyed." Here is what the Messiah is doing in you: He is creating a pure heart. He is refining your heart until it is His alone. "Give me an undivided heart," the psalmist prays (Psalm 86:11).

The Scripture says that when the Messiah appears as a refining fire, no one will be able to remain standing.

> "*Then suddenly the Lord you are seeking will come to his temple; the messenger of the covenant, whom you desire, will come,' says the Lord Almighty. But who can endure the day of*

his coming? Who can stand when he appears? For he will be
like a refiner's fire" (MALACHI 3:1–2).

When you encounter Him as the Fire from heaven, it will send you to your
knees before Him.

> *Oh, Lord, who can stand when You appear?*
> *The splendor of Your presence near*
> *Then knee must bow and tongue proclaim*
> *The pow'r of Your majestic name.*
>
> *My hungry heart cries out for You.*
> *No earthly substitute will do.*
> *Refiner's Fire, come near to me*
> *Your unveiled glory, let me see.*
>
> *A heart like Yours, my one desire.*
> *Do Your work, Refiner's Fire.*
> (POEM: JKD)

Fire Inside

The Fire that was outside in the Old Testament is inside you. You are the
tabernacle of God. You are the place where His presence is manifested and
put on display. You are where His glory dwells.

> *Your holy Fire now burns within*
> *And purges every secret sin.*
> *My life the bush, Your Life the Flame*
> *That leaves me nevermore the same.*
>
> *Your Life in me ignites the Fire*
> *That now fulfills my heart's desire.*
> *The Spirit's work, my life made new,*
> *Transformed within, ablaze with You.*
>
> *A heart like Yours, my one desire.*
> *Do Your work, Refiner's Fire.*
> (POEM: JKD)

"Do not put out the Spirit's fire" (1 Thessalonians 5:19). How brightly the fire burns depends on the depth of your surrender. The more of yourself you relinquish, the more the fire is fueled.

Each time you altar flesh, fire from heaven falls to consume it. On the altar, what was flesh becomes a sweet-smelling aroma to God. Flesh consumed releases the aroma of Christ into the world.

> *"But thanks be to God, who always leads us in triumphal procession in Christ and through us spreads everywhere the fragrance of the knowledge of him. For we are to God the aroma of Christ among those who are being saved and those who are perishing"* (2 CORINTHIANS 2:14–15).

Living in an altar'd state releases an aroma that draws those in our world to Him. Every time you choose obedience, every time you lean in to Jesus, Jesus is expressed through you and He can draw all people to Himself.

Flesh smells like flesh. Rancid, acrid, stinky. Only Jesus smells like Jesus. One repels, the other attracts. Jesus attracts people to Himself, not to you. When "you"—fleshy you—are on display, the aroma of Christ is not released.

Altar flesh and let the fire release the beautiful fragrance.

REFLECT

Invite the Refiner's Fire to do His work in you.

IN HIM I LIVE AND MOVE AND HAVE MY BEING

"I have set the Lord always before me. Because he is at my right hand, I will not be shaken" (PSALM 16:8).

As you set your mind on Him, you will find His power and His provision flowing into your life without your effort or struggle. When you make His kingdom and His righteousness your focus, everything else will be added. Your soul can live at rest when you live in an altar'd state.

When you make it your holy habit to live with an awareness of His presence in you, you will find that, at some level, you can keep Him always before you. Of course you live in the material, physical world and that's where He wants you to live. You don't have to carve out a monkish existence. You'll learn, with practice, that even while you are carrying out your day-to-day responsibilities, at another level you are interacting with Him. Your mind can do many things at one time. Some of its tasks require your full awareness and some you accomplish with barely a conscious thought. Sometimes your interaction with the Father will be at that full-awareness level, and sometimes it will be going on in the background. It doesn't matter. You find that when you are free to bring it back to your full awareness, you are just continuing an interchange of love that has been going on all along. It doesn't stop and start. It just moves from level to level of awareness, depending on the requirements of the moment. This is how you pray without ceasing (1 Thessalonians 5:17). This is how you live in His presence. This is how you live altar'd.

> *"One thing I ask of the Lord, this is what I seek: that I may dwell in the house of the Lord all the days of my life, to gaze*

upon the beauty of the Lord and to seek him in his temple"
(PSALM 27:4).

"I said to the Lord, 'You are my Lord; apart from you I have no good thing'" (Psalm 16:2). You don't need to seek any further. You've found Him, you've found everything. There is nothing good apart from Him. Surrender your heart. Altar your life. Give Him such full reign in your life that He can flood you and saturate you with His power and His presence. Nothing outside of Him is worth holding on to. Altar.

What are you clinging to? What is He trying to convince you to let go of? Are you trying to bear a burden you were not meant to carry? Are you clutching something less than His plan because it is familiar and His plan is unknown? Are you nursing anger and bitterness and resentment and refusing to let them go? Are you holding a grudge? Is there someone that sparks jealousy, envy, or competitiveness in you?

Let it go. It's deadweight. It's holding you back. It's crowding out the flow of His life. You want to run in the path of His commandments. Nothing is worth holding on to.

Learning the Landscape

Every day you are learning more how to live in an altar'd state. It has set you on a journey toward the deep things of God. As your journey takes you deeper into the kingdom, you discover that the kingdom's land formations are many and varied. Today is not like yesterday and tomorrow will not be like today—if you keep moving.

In the kingdom landscape you will find mountains and valleys one day, fertile riverland lush with foliage another. Still another day will bring you to quiet green pastures laced with gentle streams of still water. Keep moving and you may find yourself walking a well-traveled, brightly lit path, but the next day might find you on a path so untraveled and dark you feel like a blind person feeling your way step-by-step. If you plan to search out the kingdom's treasures, you will have to learn its landscape. When you do, you will not be surprised when, from time to time, you find yourself in the desert.

Desert time is not wasted. It is necessary. You have to have it. In the Scripture, desert time is transition time—laying aside old and putting on new. It is a training ground. Moses spent 40 years in the desert before he was ready to lead Israel out of Egypt. Throughout the desert time, God was preparing Moses. God was getting Moses ready to fulfill his destiny.

Are you in the desert? Have you ever been in the desert? When it's desert time, it feels like everything has dried up. It looks like there's no relief. You feel like giving up. In the desert, you learn that what *feels like* the truth and what *is* the truth are two different things.

If you're in the desert right now, you're feeling like your soul just needs rest. You've tried everything you know to try. You've searched all you can search. You've given everything you have to give.

No matter how you've tried, no matter how determined and resolved you've been, you're still in the desert. There seems to be no way out.

I want you to remember that it was in the desert that Moses encountered the Burning Bush. What appears to be a time in your life that is arid and barren is really fertile ground for a face-to-face encounter with the Living God.

God wants you to worship Him, even in the desert. "The Lord, the God of the Hebrews, has sent me to say to you: 'Let my people go, so that they may *worship me in the desert*'" (Exodus 7:16, emphasis added). To worship Him in the desert teaches you an advanced lesson in kingdom living: sometimes worshipping is an act of your will, not your emotions. Altar the flesh that keeps drawing your attention to your desert's harsh environs, and let the Spirit show you that the desert walk is taking you where you really want to go. There are some truths that become apparent only in the view from the altar.

He is "the shadow of a great rock in a thirsty land" (Isaiah 32:2). In His presence you will find relief from the draining heat and the hot, dry winds. Let yourself feel the reprieve from your circumstances as you rest in His shade. Let Him refresh you with His presence.

REFLECT

Today, at this very place in your life's journey, do you live and move and have your being in Him?

Do you find yourself focusing on your need instead of His supply?

What flesh needs to be altar'd right now, in your desert?

Day 34

DESERT GOD

G od is God of the desert. He's going to take care of you and meet your every need, but the way He meets your needs will come from the most unexpected places. If you look around you, you will see nothing but sand and rocks. No water anywhere. That's the way God wants it. He is about to teach you one of the secrets of the kingdom: what you see with your eyes is not the whole picture. Sometimes a rock is not just a rock. Sometimes a rock is really a river.

> "He split the rocks in the desert and gave them water as abundant as the seas; he brought streams out of a rocky crag and made water flow down like rivers" (PSALM 78:15–16).

When the way seems long and hot and dry; when the relentless heat of your circumstances has worn you down; when your confidence has been burned away by the desert's scorching sun — look for the Rock.

In Exodus 17:1–7 you can read the story of how God — the same God who is with you in your desert — made water gush from a rock. The Israelites were traveling in the desert and there was no water for them to drink. God told Moses to strike a certain rock with his staff. When Moses obeyed, water gushed from the rock. Enough water came from the rock to satisfy the whole nation of Israel and all their livestock. This was no trickle. This was a river. This was no drinking fountain. This was a sea of water. It was a picture of the kingdom.

> Water will gush forth in the wilderness and streams in the desert. The burning sand will become a pool, the thirsty ground bubbling springs (ISAIAH 35:6–7).

> *I will make rivers flow on barren heights, and springs within
> the valleys. I will turn the desert into pools of water, and the
> parched ground into springs* (ISAIAH 41:18).

In the symbol language of Scripture, a rock is the symbol for Jesus and
water is the Holy Spirit.

> *They all [the Israelites] . . . drank the same spiritual drink; for
> they drank from the spiritual rock that accompanied them, and
> that rock was Christ* (1 CORINTHIANS 10:3–4).

Choose your outlook: God's perspective or the perspective of your own
flesh. Which will it be? This decision will change your desert experience.
If you choose to whine and snivel your way through the desert, it will be a
draining trek. If you choose to lay hold of the truth, you will find the water
that gushes from the Rock.

Honest to God

If you felt that you could be 100 percent honest, would you say you feel
angry with God for bringing you into the desert? It's OK to be angry with
God. He isn't angry with you. He knows how you feel and why you feel it.
Sometimes that feeling of being frustrated with God is actually a statement
of faith: If you didn't think that God was in control, you'd have nothing to
feel angry with Him about! So let your anger and frustration be proof to
your own heart of your faith. That's how God sees it.

You can tell God exactly how you feel. He knows anyway. He wants
you to express yourself to Him because it opens the way for Him to express
Himself to you. He knows all about you. The secrets of your heart are an
open book to Him. Unlike human beings, God does not react angrily to
your anger. He loves you with a love that is not fragile. You can't make Him
not love you. There's nothing you can think or feel that will make Him not
love you.

Surrendering your flesh to crucifixion doesn't mean pretending. In
fact, it requires stark honesty. You don't have to have acceptable feelings all
the time to make God love you. He has given His Son for you, and given
His Son to you. Nothing will make Him withdraw His love from you.

Flesh pretends and hides and disguises. Spirit puts it all out in the light. You can't altar what you can't see or admit.

You have to come to a place where you can accept that you are in the desert and that you'll be in the desert until God brings you out. You have to embrace the desert. You have to choose to believe that God is working good things into you life while you're in the desert. Are you there?

See if these words express your heart: "Lord, even though I feel tired and discouraged, even though I can't see You anywhere in my circumstances, I'm making a choice right now to believe You are here. I'm going to stop trying to get out of the desert and, instead, I'm going to look for the Rock."

Could this be a statement of your faith? "I'm in the desert and I can't get myself out. So I'm going to be in the desert until God brings me out on the other side. I won't always be in the desert, but while I'm here, I'm going to surrender to whatever God is doing in me, even if I don't know what that is. I'm going to learn to thrive in the desert. I'm going to live in a altar'd state."

The desert is the place where God can create in you a thirst for Him. In the desert, God will teach you a craving for Him and His presence.

> *As the deer pants for streams of water, so my soul pants for you, O God. My soul thirsts for God, for the living God. When can I go and meet with God?* (Psalm 42:1–2).

> *O God, you are my God, earnestly I seek you; my soul thirsts for you, my body longs for you, in a dry and weary land where there is no water* (Psalm 63:1).

In the desert, God develops in you a heart that will settle for nothing less than *all* of Him. He creates an intense longing for Him that opens your life to His presence. He teaches you that nothing else will satisfy you. Your soul thirsts for Living Water. He lets that thirst grow and grow until it defines your life. He makes you thirsty so He can satisfy your soul with Himself.

REFLECT

Are you in the desert? What is God working out in your desert?

Let your thirst grow. When your flesh serves up desperation, altar it and find it turned into thirst.

Day 35
THE JOY OF THE LORD

One of the hallmarks of Jesus' life is joy. Unbridled, unrestrained joy. And flesh can't counterfeit it. Though flesh promises joy, it can't deliver. "If you just do this, buy that, say the other, you would feel happy." Now, certainly your flesh doesn't talk. It doesn't form those sentences. But think about the patterns your flesh has developed. Why do you repeat behavior that has in the past proven unfruitful? Something in you believes that you just have to act in that flesh pattern one more time and this time it will bring happiness, or peace, or contentment, or whatever you are trying to squeeze out of it.

Joy marks the life of person whose heart belongs exclusively to Jesus. Joy is impossible to define. It can be known only by experiencing it. Joy is an emotion that comes out of your spirit . The flesh has a shadow version of joy called happiness or pleasure. But the flesh's version is flat, one-dimensional and transitory. Unlike happiness, which comes and goes with circumstances, joy is spiritual. Joy is in effect continually because it is based on the solid and unchanging life of Jesus.

The joy that a Spirit-led Christian experiences is the very joy of the indwelling Christ being expressed through his personality. Jesus, in His prayer recorded in John 17, said that everything He was asking from the Father on behalf of His disciples was "so that they may have the full measure of my joy within them" (John 17:13). Let me restate this sentence. "Father, let My followers be filled to the brim and overflowing with the joy that I possess. I will be in them, pouring My own joy into their hearts."

The heart that has passed through crucifixion and is continually altaring flesh is able to receive the rivers of joy flowing toward it. When you and I are experiencing joy, it is His joy we are experiencing. Joy has no other source. "All my springs of joy are in you" (Psalm 87:7 NASB).

Joy, because it is based in eternal truth instead of momentary events, is always available to the believer, no matter what circumstance confronts him. Flesh blocks the flow of joy; flesh causes the heart to be resistant to joy. Flesh focuses on the situation as it appears from the earthly perspective; the flesh attributes power to circumstances. The flesh's earthbound perspective interrupts the flow of joy. However, the Spirit-saturated heart is filled with joy in every circumstance. Your spirit transfused with His life looks at every circumstance in the light of His presence. In that light, you are able to see circumstances from a new perspective. Factors once hidden in shadow are now exposed. More of the full picture is in view. And it is framed in the goodness and the sovereignty of God.

> Child, I know all about the situation that is worrying you right now. I knew about it before you did. Believe me when I tell you it is finished. Your prayers are bringing the finished work out of the spiritual realm to establish it in the material realm. You do not see the finished work in the earth environment yet, but earth is not your home. Do you know why you are having difficulty believing right now? Because you have only looked at the situation in the artificial light of the earth kingdom. Earth kingdom's light only shows up the need. Bring it to Me. Spend time with Me in your true kingdom. Look at it in the Eternal Light. I will blot out the need and illumine only the supply. Come!
>
> (*The Secret Place of the Most High*, Jennifer Kennedy Dean)

If you could see His whole plan from beginning to end, see His purposes and His heart, see how this very circumstance was being used for long-term profit, then you would choose to be right where you are. It all comes down to this one thing: Him. You can be filled with uninterrupted joy because of who He is. "May all who seek you rejoice and be glad in you; may those who love your salvation always say, 'Let God be exalted!'" (Psalm 40:7).

Joyful Jesus

Jesus is filled with joy. We are mistaken to think that, in His earthly visage, He was somber, stern and melancholy. The Scripture paints Him as witty and outgoing and charismatic and winsome. Children loved to be with

Him. He was invited to parties. In fact, His enemies criticized Him for having too much fun.

> *"For John the Baptist came neither eating bread nor drinking wine, and you say 'He has a demon.' The Son of Man came eating and drinking, and you say, 'Here is a glutton and a drunkard, a friend of tax collectors and sinners'"* (LUKE 7:33–34).

When God became flesh—when Jesus made the Father known—He showed us that the Father is filled with joy.

The joyful Jesus lives in me and in you. He is living His joy from His dwelling place in your innermost being. His plan is that you will be the conduit through which He expresses His joy. He wants His joy to be in you and He wants your joy to be complete. The Greek word translated "complete" means to be filled to the brim so that nothing is lacking. He wants you to have the fullness of His joy.

"I have told you these things so that my joy may be in you and your joy may be complete" (John 15:11). What did Jesus tell us that would result in being filled with His joy?

> *"As the Father has loved me, so have I loved you. Now remain in my love. If you obey my commands, you will remain in my love, just as I have obeyed my Father's commands and remain in his love. I have told you this so that my joy may be in you and that your joy may be complete"* (JOHN 15:9–11).

The key to seeing His joy flow in and through you? Obedience.

Anointed with the Oil of Joy

He wants to pour His joy into you. His joy is based on His knowledge of the Father. He knows that the Father is always working according to an eternal plan, a plan that has a good, productive and beneficial outcome. He knows that nothing occurs outside of the Father's sovereignty and that He can always rejoice in what the Father is bringing about.

When His life flows through you, His faith flows through you; His joy flows through you; His strength flows through you. What is facing you right now? Do you think that Jesus is worried about it and anxious about it? Or do you think that Jesus is absolutely certain that this circumstance is positioning you and preparing you for the fullness of the Spirit and for the next step in the Father's plan? Yield yourself to His Life within you. Let Him fill you full of His joy even in the midst of difficult circumstances. Lean in. Live in an altar'd state.

RESPOND

Offer Him your difficult circumstances as avenues through which to display His power. Let your surrender be an act of worship, in spirit and in truth. The Father is seeking such worshippers.

JOY, JOY, JOY DOWN IN MY HEART

"You have filled my heart with greater joy than when their grain and new wine abound" (Psalm 4:7). The joy that flows from Jesus into your heart is outside of and beyond circumstances. It is a joy that surpasses the happiness that earthly success brings. True joy is so Christ-centered that earthly success can neither add to it nor diminish it.

Success in the earthly realm is not wrong. In fact, it is a gift from God and He wants you to enjoy it with Him. In the Old Covenant, God established the Feast of Tabernacles as a seven-day celebration of the harvest. His instructions are:

> "For seven days celebrate the Feast to the Lord your God at the place the Lord will choose. For the Lord your God will bless you in all your harvest and in all the work of your hands, and your joy will be complete" (DEUTERONOMY 16:15).

Do you recognize the phrasing? Jesus used the same words: "that Your joy will be complete." God wants you to take great pleasure in what He provides and to find joy in it because you know it came from Him.

However, there will be other times when His blessings and His favor do not come in material, financial, or physical form. There will be times when from the point of view of earth it will appear that God is withholding His blessing. There will be times when your circumstances seem not to be the platform for God's power. Then what?

> "Though the fig tree does not bud and there are no grapes on the vines, though the olive crop fails and the fields produce no

food, though there are no sheep in the pen and no cattle in the
stalls, yet I will rejoice in the Lord, I will be joyful in God my
Savior" (HABAKKUK 3:16–18).

Joy, when it is truly joy, will not abandon you even then. Under the surface
of your emotions you will discover a strong undercurrent of joy. It is His
joy. It is eternal; it is changeless; it is His gift to you. It is yours when you
live in an altar'd state.

You can rejoice because you know that God is in control. You can
rejoice because you know that God is working everything out for His
good purposes. You can rejoice in advance for what God will do. You
can rejoice because you know that nothing is too difficult for Him and
nothing is impossible to Him. You can rejoice because He is doing
something that is beyond what you can ask or even imagine. You can
rejoice *in the Lord.*

A Life of Praise

"My soul will be satisfied as with the richest of foods; with singing lips my
mouth will praise you" (Psalm 63:5). Joy expresses itself in praise. Praise
is the spontaneous and natural outflow of the inflow of His Life. When my
soul is satisfied as if it had feasted on the richest of foods, when my soul
is flooded with His Life, then praise spills over. Altar'd living flows with
spontaneous praise.

Praise completes the experience of joy. The more my soul is filled
with Him, the more of His joy that floods me, the more "my mouth is
filled with [His] praise" (Psalm 71:8) and "my lips overflow with praise"
(Psalm 119:171).

The key to true joy, we've seen, is that it is joy in the Lord. The key
to authentic praise is that it is the expression of a satisfied soul. The soul
can only be satisfied with the presence of God through the indwelling life
of Christ because that is its destiny. Because God has "set eternity in the
hearts of men" (Ecclesiastes 3:11), nothing less than eternity—nothing
temporal—will satisfy. God says, "I will fill the soul of the priests with
abundance, And My people shall be satisfied with My goodness" (Jeremiah
31:14 NASB). The word translated "fill" means to saturate. He will saturate
our souls (we are priests according to 1 Peter 2:5, 9) with His abundance
and it will satisfy us. His abundance will satiate that soul-craving that is

born into us. And when our souls are satisfied as if they had dined on the richest food, praise will instinctively flow.

What is His abundance? What is His richest treasure and His satisfying, nourishing food? Jesus. Where is Jesus? In you.

Not only will praise complete the experience of joy, but it will also multiply the joy. In the times when your emotions are at their lowest and when the joy of the Lord seems faint, begin to offer praise. Your freewill offering of praise will put your flesh on the cross because praise is the deathblow to self-life. Praise is one of the best tools for altaring. Your decision to offer praise will give the Spirit ascendancy over your flesh. Praise is one of the most powerful weapons in your war against flesh life. How do you live in an altar'd state when things seem dark? Choose life. Praise.

As you genuinely praise God, basing your praise on truth, though it begins as a deliberate act on your part, it is very likely to turn into praise that engages your emotions and begins to open them to be filled with Jesus' joy. Again, joy is a work of the Spirit and its indestructibility will astound you. Live in an altar'd state and you will find that joy meets you there.

Praise That Fits

> "Sing joyfully to the Lord, you righteous; it is fitting for the upright to praise him" (PSALM 33:1).

Praise fits you. And praise fits God. Praise is fitting—appropriate, right, suitable.

As you praise, you are releasing tremendous spiritual power. Praise dispels the enemy's troops. Praise lays the groundwork for the display of God's power. "He who sacrifices thank offerings honors me, and he prepares the way so that I may show him the salvation of God" (Psalm 50:23).

"God inhabits the praises of His people" (Psalm 22:3 KJV). The praises of His people have God's Life in them. In the spiritual realm, we are always the responders and the receivers and God is always the initiator and the giver. This is even so in praise. It is the Spirit of the Son in us who is stirring up praise, who is bringing to our thoughts all the reasons that God is worthy of our praise, who is expressing His joy through our praise. When I praise God it is really the Son praising through me. I am speaking the words of praise that He is speaking in me. His words coming through my mouth have the Life of God in them because His words are life. The praises of God's people have God's Life in them; He inhabits the praises of His people. Genuine praise rises from the altar'd life.

Praise is fitting. I was created "for the praise of his glory" (Ephesians 1:6, 12) so that when my life is praising Him I am fulfilling my destiny. Praise fits me.

Praise fits God. "Great is the Lord and most worthy of praise; his greatness no one can fathom" (Psalm 145:3). He is worthy of praise. You have, I'm sure, had the experience of being around a person who needed an inordinate amount of praise and who sought it constantly. It is an uncomfortable situation and becomes wearying. Or you've had the experience of yourself being praised far beyond what was necessary or deserved. It is also an uncomfortable situation. In these cases, the praise is not fitting. The object of praise is not worthy. Only God is worthy. Praising God, who is worthy to be praised, is invigorating instead of wearying because it is fitting.

Praise releases faith. As you praise God, keeping the eyes of your heart focused on Him, you find that faith is present in you. Praise keeps you centered in Him. It keeps your attention on the Supply rather than the need. When your attention is fixed on Him, problems, needs, circumstances all take on their proper perspective.

RESPOND

Altar yourself. Take time to consciously allow the Spirit of the Son in you to stir up praise. Be aware of this spiritual dynamic. Spend an extended time in praise. Write it; speak it; sing it. Let the altar do its work in you.

Day 37
REST FOR YOUR SOUL

F lesh is always working. Flesh can't rest because it feels responsible and it can't stop trying to get things lined up as the flesh thinks they should be. Flesh can't hand things over. Flesh has to stay in charge. Flesh can't live in the restful state that God has available for us.

Are anxiety, fear, and stress your constant companions? Does uncertainty dog your way? Are you plagued with feelings of insecurity? Is your soul in a state of turmoil? The Father wants to take you by the hand and lead you into His rest, just as He took Israel by the hand to lead her out of Egypt and unto the Land of Rest (Jeremiah 31:32). He wants to teach you that Sabbath is not a day of the week but a state of the soul. He wants you to know the secret of living in a soul sabbath.

> "Come to me, all you who are weary and burdened, and I will give you rest. Take my yoke upon you and learn from me, for I am gentle and humble in heart, and you will find rest for your souls. For my yoke is easy and my burden is light"
> (MATTHEW 11:28–30).

What your flesh cannot offer, Jesus gives freely. He is your soul's safe place, your resting place. His life in you is the solid rock on which you can lean all the weight of your life and its burdens and needs. If you want to learn to live in a soul sabbath, learn to live in a altar'd state. Lean in.

The Old Testament is a book of shadows, the substance of which is revealed in the New Testament. Everything recorded in the Old Testament Scriptures is true and accurate. The events recorded there really happened, and the spiritual principles are authentic, but running through the whole document is another layer of truth. Everything points to Jesus. Jesus is central in every page of the Old Covenant: He is the substance Whose shadow is cast from Genesis through Malachi. As we begin to look for the substance of the "sabbath rest" in the Old Testament, keep this principle in mind: a shadow is a one-dimensional drawing of the reality. It is not the whole picture. It is a signpost pointing to the reality.

Often, at the first mention of an idea, certain foundational truths are introduced, upon which further revelation will build. For sabbath, the first mention is in Genesis 2:1–3. Because I want the language to be an exact translation from the original Hebrew, I quote this passage from *The Five Books of Moses* by Everett Fox.

> "Thus were finished the heavens and the earth, with all of their array. God had finished, on the seventh day, his work that he had made, and then he ceased, on the seventh day, from all his work that he had made. God gave the seventh day his blessing, and he hallowed it, for on it he ceased from all his work, that by creating, God had made."

The Hebrew word that Fox translated "ceased" is the word *shabbat*. The word in English is the same root from which the noun Sabbath *comes*. In most of our translations, the word has been translated "rest." Notice that Fox translated *shabbat* as "cease" rather than "rest." In Genesis 2:2, then, we find that God "sabbathed."

Why did God rest on the seventh day? Had He exhausted Himself? The Scripture is clear: God rested because He was finished. He was finished with all of His work, so He sabbathed. He ceased. The word *shabbat* means "to be finished; to have completed the work."

God created for six days, and then He sabbathed. For how long did He sabbath? Did He pick up where He'd left off when Day Eight dawned? God, on the seventh day of creation, began a sabbath that was to last forever. "And yet his work has been finished since the creation of the world" (Hebrews 4:3).

From a heavenly viewpoint, God's work has been in a finished state, completed, since day seven. When was the Lamb slain? Before the world began (Revelation 13:8). When were the names of those who would be saved written in the book of life? Before the world began (Revelation 17:8; Ephesians 1:4). When was the kingdom prepared for believers? Before the world began (Matthew 25:34). Look at:

- 2 Thessalonians 2:13
- 2 Timothy 1:9
- Titus 1:1–2
- Ephesians 2:10

All of His work was finished, and so He sabbathed.

Yet Jesus stated, "'My Father is always at his work to this very day, and I, too, am working'" (John 5:17). At one level, everything is finished. God's work in its finished state is on the spiritual end of the continuum. The work left to do is to release it into the material end of the continuum in the fullness of time.

> *"This grace was given us in Christ Jesus before the beginning of time, but it has now been revealed through the appearing of our Savior, Christ Jesus, who has destroyed death and has brought life and immortality to light through the gospel"* (2 Timothy 1:9–10).

Do you see what this means? The action—grace was given us in Christ Jesus—was completed before the beginning of time. But God revealed it in Christ's coming to earth. God's work is finished, but it will be revealed on the earth at its ripe and appointed moment. What Jesus is doing in us now is revealing on the earth what God has already finished in heaven.

The Sabbath Day Observance

God established the Sabbath day, the seventh day of each week, to be set aside for rest from work and for delighting in the Lord. The Sabbath observance is a day on which His people are to mimic His rest. We are to enter into peaceful tranquility, the perpetual state of the Father. The scientific community provides ample proof that regular rest from work is necessary for the mental and physical well-being of persons, animals, and land. The observance of the Sabbath rest is beneficial to the physical world and provides for its optimum functioning. But the physical and mental rest of the Sabbath observance is only a shadow of the real rest and soul sabbath that God has made available to His people. Let me say again, sabbath is not ultimately a day of the week, but a state of the soul.

The Land of Rest

The next shadow figure of sabbath rest is the Promised Land. The state of rest in the Garden of Eden was disrupted by the entrance of sin. It began as a land of rest, but became a place of labor, turmoil, and death. When God promised His people a land of their own, He called it a land of rest. Part of the gift of land was the gift of rest. "Come into Canaan. This is where I will give you rest," is essentially the invitation of Yahweh to His people.

> *"You are not to do as we do here today, everyone as he sees fit, since you have not yet reached the resting place and the inheritance the LORD your God is giving you. But you will cross the Jordan and settle in the land the LORD your God is giving you as an inheritance, and he will give you rest from all your enemies around you so that you will live in safety"* (DEUTERONOMY 12:8–10).

> *"Praise be to the LORD, who has given rest to his people Israel just as he promised. Not one word has failed of all the good promises he gave through his servant Moses"* (1 KINGS 8:56).

The Promised Land, the land of Canaan, the homeland, was to be a land of rest. Rest from enemies, rest from uncertainty, rest from striving. Physical rest and soul rest. In the land of Canaan, God's people could live in His rest. When the nation of Israel refused to enter the land because of fear, God said of them:

> *"For forty years I was angry with that generation; I said, 'They are a people whose hearts go astray, and they have not known my ways.' So I declared on oath in my anger, 'They shall never enter my rest'"* (PSALM 95:10–11).

At this point, then, we have sabbath (God's rest), celebrated and remembered by a weekly observance and represented by a land. Sabbath is God's rest into which His people may enter. Canaan is His rest. When His people entered Canaan, it was God's intent that they enter a land where the work had been finished.

> "When the LORD your God brings you into the land he swore
> to your fathers, to Abraham, Isaac and Jacob, to give you — a
> land with large, flourishing cities you did not build, houses
> filled with all kinds of good things you did not provide, wells
> you did not dig, and vineyards and olive groves you did not
> plant — then when you eat and are satisfied, be careful that
> you do not forget the LORD" (DEUTERONOMY 6:10–12).

Canaan in the material realm is a geographical location. At the other end
of the continuum, in the spiritual realm, it is Jesus Himself. The Promised
Land is the shadow of the Promised One. The writer of Hebrews connected
these pictures, making them one thought: Sabbath, Canaan, God's rest,
and Jesus. In Hebrews 3:16–4:10, the writer makes the case as follows.
This is my summary of this passage:

> Quoting Psalm 95:7–11, the writer reminded his readers of "the
> rebellion" or "the testing." The incident referred to is found in Exodus
> 17:1–7 when the Israelites complained against God and against
> Moses because there was no water. Having seen God provide
> miraculously for their every single need, they still did not trust God to
> meet their new needs as they arose. This is when God swore that
> this generation would never enter His rest (Canaan). The Israelites
> did not experience the rest of Canaan because of their unbelief.
> They trusted their own perceptions (flesh) more than they trusted
> God's Word.

The writer immediately moved the analogy to the present, in essence
warning readers: Don't let the same thing happen to you. You can
experience Christ (the real Canaan) if you operate in faith as need enters
your life (Hebrews 3:7–19).

The same good news of a promised rest has been given to us. The
Israelites' promise was Canaan; our promise is Jesus. They did not partake
of the rest because the promise they received was not combined with
faith — they did not act confidently on the promise. But the promise still
remains. We can enter into the rest, and, in fact, those who have believed
have entered the Promised Land, the place of rest — Jesus (4:1–3). We can
lean in to the present indwelling Jesus.

The Scripture tells us that God rested on the seventh day; then it says, "'They shall never enter my rest,'" tying God's Sabbath rest to the Promised Land (4:4–5). Then,

> *"For if Joshua had given them rest [in Canaan], God would not have spoken later about another day. There remains, then, a Sabbath-rest for the people of God; for anyone who enters God's rest also rests from his own work, just as God did from his"* (HEBREWS 4:8–10).

Again, God's own eternal sabbath, based on His finished work, was pictured by Canaan. Just as the Israelites could enter Canaan, we can "enter God's rest." Jesus is Canaan. Jesus is the finished work. Jesus is sabbath. Jesus is rest.

What does sabbath mean for us?

Sabbath for you and me means living our lives in absolute surrender and total trust in the finished work of Christ. Not only is the salvation work finished in Him, but every need that comes into our lives has already been provided for; every dilemma has already been resolved; every question has already been answered. We simply have to place our lives in the flow of His provision. Abide in Christ. Live where the power is operating. Live in an altar'd state. Faith-born obedience puts us in the land where the soul has continual sabbath rest. Hear Him saying, "Come to Me. Learn from Me. You will find rest for your soul." The more you learn from Him, the easier it will be to rest in Him.

RESPOND

Let your mind rest in the powerful presence of the indwelling Jesus. Let the supernatural peace that radiates from Him saturate your soul. Let Him so fill you with thoughts of Himself that no room is left for anxiety.

HISTORY LESSONS

A s we approach the last days of this course, I want to wrap it all up by pointing to illustrations in Scripture that play out the whole picture of altar'd flesh—crucifixion followed by resurrection. God has worked this message into His Word from the beginning. It is not a new message. Watch how God has been portraying this reality in the lives of His people.

When God puts gifts and provision into our lives, often our flesh gets all wrapped around them. We start thinking we own them. We start thinking we should get the credit for them. We start thinking they should define us. Our flesh has to be circumcised—cut off. Your flesh wants to own and control and possess and manage and manipulate. God is always working in you to free you of your flesh and move you more and more into the power of the Spirit. To that end, He arranges crisis moments at which you are brought face-to-face with your flesh and the claim it is trying to have on God's provision. Those times are painful, but they are the most productive times of all.

Moses' Parents

The writer of Hebrews spotlighted Moses' parents as prime examples of how faith works. The call of Moses began as a vision in the minds of his parents, who *saw* that he was no ordinary child. God caused them to see His promise and hope jumped up and took such possession of them that a bold and reckless faith was born, freeing them from fear of the pharaoh. They didn't know all its ramifications, but their vision was that he would live and not die at the pharaoh's hands. That may be as far as they could see, but it was far enough.

God had to have provided supernatural protection for the baby Moses. He gave wisdom and ideas to Moses' parents. Why did they even think that a little ark of bulrushes might protect Moses' life? How did the idea even occur to them? They surely weren't the first Hebrew parents to try to save their son.

Three months they loved him and nurtured him and memorized his darling face and recorded in their hearts his dear sighs and gurgles and cries. With each passing day, love grew.

When the day came to let him go, imagine his mother's walk from her home to the Nile's edge. Three-month-old son entombed in a basket.

Surely only her selfless love for her son could induce her to walk her Via Dolorosa (Way of the Cross). Had she given one thought to her own desires, she would have turned back. She was going to place him into the Nile in the days when the Nile ran red with the blood of Hebrew sons. She was letting him go into the river that his enemy had declared to be his burial place. Imagine as she stood in the Nile's waters and came to that moment when she had to do the hardest thing she would ever be called upon to do. She had to let him go. She had to die to her mother's instincts to guard and protect. To save his life, she had to let him go.

When she did, her son was put upon the course he had been ordained to travel. The very river that might have been his end was instead his beginning. His mother received him back again, but everything had changed. When she put him into the Nile he was a slave. When she received him back from the Nile, he was a prince. Crucifixion, resurrection.

The secret was in the letting go her altar'd state allowed Moses to come fully into his destiny.

Moses

Moses was among the most powerful men in Egypt. Mighty in both word and action. Positioned to rule Egypt. Strong, handsome, intelligent, highly educated. Moses had it all.

Moses was also pregnant with promise. An inner vision kept seeping into his thinking and his passions and grew stronger with each passing year. He wanted his Hebrew kinsmen to be free. As the vision gestated and grew more substantive, Moses realized that he wanted to be the one to free them. Then came the day when Moses tried to give birth to the vision prematurely. He tried to induce labor. He murdered an Egyptian taskmaster who was beating a Hebrew slave. At best—if all had gone well—Moses would have temporarily rescued one lone Hebrew. He would have rescued one slave from one taskmaster for one day. Do you see how far short that falls of the vision that God had in mind? Do you see what a cheap imitation we produce when the vision gets tangled up with our flesh?

When Moses happened upon this incident, he must have thought, "This is my chance. It's now or never. When I strike this blow, all my Hebrew kinsmen will recognize that I can set them free." Notice how Stephen reports it in Acts 7:25–26. "Moses thought that his own people would realize that God was using him to rescue them, but they did not."

Moses had no qualms about his ability to rescue Israel. He had no doubt that, not only could he accomplish it, but also that the people would recognize and embrace him as their rescuer. He probably thought, "Of course God has chosen and appointed me to rescue Israel. Who else? I'm the only one who could accomplish it. Anyone can see that I am the man." Moses was absolutely confident in Moses. Moses trusted in Moses.

Then Moses experienced something that he had never experienced before in his life. Failure. Humiliation. And he was doing what God had, from all eternity, set him in place to do. But he was doing it in his flesh.

This incident in Moses' life was all part of God's plan for how the call would develop. Moses' failure was not a setback, but was a step forward in the gestation of the call. Even our failures, when surrendered to the purposes of God, turn out to be essential to the development of the promise. Because of His failure, Moses' life was open to God for a new work. Now God could take Moses' strength and make it weakness, so that He could take Moses' weakness and make it strength. When we are weak, then we are strong.

When God came to Moses 40 years later, and called him to rescue Israel—the Moses who once thought that it should be obvious to anyone that he was the rescuer no longer lived. A new Moses had been born. This Moses said, "'Who am I, that I should go to Pharaoh and bring the Israelites out of Egypt?' And God said, 'I will be with you'" (Exodus 3:11–12). From that moment, all of the exodus event emphasizes, not who Moses is, but who God is.

God implanted the promise in Moses from his birth. He formed Moses and timed his appearance on earth for just this purpose. He grew and nourished the vision in Moses. And then He circumcised the vision. He cut away all of Moses' flesh from the promise and left it with nothing but God.

When Moses went into Egypt and persevered in what God told him to do, through what looked like setbacks, and humiliations, and the doubts of his people, he was in an altar'd state. God had used the desert years to do deep crucifixion work so resurrection power could operate full throttle.

It's All in the Staff

In the desert years, Moses — now a shepherd — had a staff. His staff was what he leaned on. His staff was what he counted on for his work. His staff was his strength.

When God called Moses at the burning bush, His first command was, "Throw it on the ground." God called Moses to take that which he leaned on for strength and throw it down before the LORD. You know the story. It turned into a snake. Maybe it was revealing its true nature. Then, God commanded Moses to pick it up again, and it turned back into a staff. "'This,' said the LORD, 'is so that they may believe that the LORD, the God of their fathers — the God of Abraham, the God of Isaac and the God of Jacob — has appeared to you'" (Exodus 4:5).

Now how does that make sense? The people weren't there to see the incident. They would never believe Moses' story about what happened How could that private moment between Moses and God serve as the proof to the people that Moses had met God?

From then on, the staff was God's means of acting through Moses. It was not Moses' staff anymore, it was God's. "So Moses . . . took the staff of God in his hand" (Exodus 4:20). The miraculous power that God displayed through Moses involved his staff. Staff held out over the Red Sea. Staff held up to bring victory in battle. Staff used to combat the Pharaoh. "But take this staff in your hand so you can perform miraculous signs with it" (Exodus 4:17). The staff had not changed its physical appearance. It looked on the outside exactly the same as it had before. But it had been transformed. It was another staff altogether. The old staff had passed away and Moses' staff had become a new creation. That transformation allowed Moses, who once had tried to rescue Israel with his own brute strength, to prove to his kinsmen that, though the outside had not changed, the inside was brand new.

When we live our lives in an altar'd state, Christ's life will be made visible to those around us. What is it you have been leaning on? Throw it down. Lean in to the indwelling present powerful Jesus. He will be your staff, your strength.

REFLECT

What's in your basket as you stand in your Nile River?

What staff are you leaning on when you need to throw it down?

Day 39

GENERATIONAL FLESH

Like Moses, Jacob was a man who had great natural strength. He was skillful at molding circumstances and manipulating events to bring about the outcome he desired. He trusted in the strength of his flesh. God intended to use Jacob to fulfill His plan (Genesis 28:13–14), but Jacob's flesh-strength had to be crucified before the power of God could be put on display in him.

Joseph had lived by the strength of his flesh all his life, it seems. His flesh seemed to serve him well. He took advantage of his older twin brother, Esau, when Esau was in need and convinced his older brother to turn over his birthright to Jacob before he would help. He seemed to know how to hone in on Esau's weakness and turn it to serve his purposes. Then, as his aged and blind father lay dying, Jacob disguised himself as his hairy older brother and, again, stole the blessing of the firstborn through deceit. His flesh excelled at deceiving.

Notice that everything he achieved through deceit and trickery, were things God intended to give him in his life. God told Jacob's mother while he was still in the womb: "The LORD said to her, 'Two nations are in your womb, and two peoples from within you will be separated; one people will be stronger than the other, and the older will serve the younger'" (Genesis 25:23). Before he was born, God had already foretold His own plan for Jacob. Do you remember flesh's nature? Flesh wants to be its own source. Flesh wants to provide for itself what only God can provide. Though Jacob seemed to be successful in his flesh's accomplishments, that success carried in it the seeds of his own downfall.

Doing things his own way, Jacob set himself up to be tricked and deceived. Forced from his homeland because of Esau's wrath—brought on by Jacob's tricks—Jacob found himself at the mercy of his uncle Laban, who apparently had Jacob's same flavor of flesh. He hoaxed Jacob as Jacob had done to his father and his brother. He tricked Jacob into marrying his older daughter Leah when Jacob believed himself to be marrying his beloved Rebekah. Laban's deceit of Jacob is almost a retelling of Jacob's deceit of his father. Jacob pretended to be Esau to gain position; Laban had Leah pretend to be Rebekah to gain position. Sow to the flesh; reap from the flesh. When the flesh promises to obtain for you what only God can give, it delivers an inferior product. A cheap imitation that wears thin and wears out.

The vision that God has for your life is something you desire. You were born for it. You are supposed to long for it. The danger is that we will try to bring it about in the power of our flesh. We might have enough success in the power of our flesh that we come to trust it. It takes a while for things to unravel.

Notice the flesh that flowed through generations. Laban was Jacob's mother Rebekahs' brother. It was Rebekah who planned the deceit of her husband, tricking him into thinking Jacob was Esau. The story is recorded in Genesis 27:1–30. Throughout the story, you see that the plot is complex. There are several hurdles to get over, but Rebekah has already thought them through. She first overheard Isaac—Jacob's father—that he was ready to bless Esau, and after overhearing that conversation, she made her devious plan.

She is the one who laid it all out for Jacob. She had Jacob bring her goats so she could prepare Isaac's favorite meal. Rebekah gathered Esau's clothes for Jacob, and Rebekah thought of covering the smooth-faced Jacob with goatskins so that if Isaac reached out to touch his son, he would mistake him for hairy Esau. All this was very detailed and took much thought and planning. It was genius, really. This seems to me to be a person to whom scheming came naturally. I'm guessing now, but I'm basing my guess on what the Scripture tells us about this bloodline that ran through Jacob from Rebekah. I'm guessing that Rebekah used trickery and manipulation often. It seems to have come easily to her. She passed that flesh on to Jacob, and we see a strong strain of it in her brother Laban.

This incredible bent toward deceiving went on even after Laban had tricked Jacob into marrying Leah. When Jacob made plans to leave Laban and start his own flock, dueling deceitfulness created such a convoluted situation that I think you need to read it for yourself. From Genesis 30:29–43:

Jacob said to him, "You know how I have worked for you and how your livestock has fared under my care. The little you had before I came has increased greatly, and the LORD has blessed you wherever I have been. But now, when may I do something for my own household?"

"What shall I give you?" he asked. "Don't give me anything," Jacob replied. "But if you will do this one thing for me, I will go on tending your flocks and watching over them:

"Let me go through all your flocks today and remove from them every speckled or spotted sheep, every dark-colored lamb and every spotted or speckled goat. They will be my wages. And my honesty will testify for me in the future, whenever you check on the wages you have paid me. Any goat in my possession that is not speckled or spotted, or any lamb that is not dark-colored, will be considered stolen."

"Agreed," said Laban. "Let it be as you have said."

That same day he removed all the male goats that were streaked or spotted, and all the speckled or spotted female goats (all that had white on them) and all the dark-colored lambs, and he placed them in the care of his sons.

Then he put a three-day journey between himself and Jacob, while Jacob continued to tend the rest of Laban's flocks. Jacob, however, took fresh-cut branches from poplar, almond and plane trees and made white stripes on them by peeling the bark and exposing the white inner wood of the branches.

Then he placed the peeled branches in all the watering troughs, so that they would be directly in front of the flocks when they came to drink. When the flocks were in heat and came to drink, they mated in front of the branches. And they bore young that were streaked or speckled or spotted. Jacob set apart the young of the flock by themselves, but made the rest face the streaked and dark-colored animals that belonged to Laban. Thus he made separate flocks for himself and did not put them with Laban's animals.

Whenever the stronger females were in heat, Jacob would place the branches in the troughs in front of the animals so they would mate near the branches, but if the animals were weak, he would not place them there. So the weak animals went to

Laban and the strong ones to Jacob. In this way the man grew exceedingly prosperous and came to own large flocks, and maidservants and menservants, and camels and donkeys.

One deceiver outdoing the other. Flesh flows through generations until one generation learns the secret of living in an altar'd state. Might it be that when you learn to altar your flesh, generations change?

Winning Through Losing

For Jacob, the defining moment—the crucifixion moment—came at a place Jacob named Peniel.

Jacob, having sent his family and his servants ahead, was alone. God came to Jacob in the form of a man and wrestled with him all night long. I want you to notice that God approached Jacob and initiated this wrestling match. The goal of a wrestling match is to have your opponent flat on the ground and helpless. Jacob resisted God and would not surrender, so greatly did he value his flesh strength. But God, determined to bring Jacob to the place of victory, reached out and "touched the socket of Jacob's hip so that his hip was wrenched as he wrestled" (Genesis 32:25).

The hip joint is the strongest joint in the human body. The thigh muscle is the strongest muscle in the human body. God broke Jacob at the point of his strength. The wrestling match was over. Jacob, now broken and helpless, said to God, "I will not let you go unless you bless me" (v. 26). Jacob at his strongest could not have held God captive. Certainly in his brokenness he could not. Yet the Scripture seems to imply that God could not leave Jacob. Do you know why I think it was? It was not that God did not have the *strength* to break Jacob's grip; it is that He did not have the *heart* to break Jacob's grip. When in his brokenness and helplessness Jacob clung to God and cried out to Him from the depths of his own weakness, God declared Jacob a winner. "Your name will no longer be Jacob, but Israel, because you have struggled with God and with men and have overcome" (v. 28). When did God say Jacob had won? When he lost. When I am weak, then I am strong.

Altar'd living proves the power of the indwelling Christ. At the point of my brokenness, the power of Christ is on full display.

REFLECT

Where is your hip joint? Can you see God's determination to let you win by losing? Will you altar yourself?

ABRAHAM'S CRUCIFIXION

A braham's faith is described in the Book of Hebrews, held out as an eternal example of how to live by faith. To see this principle of circumcising the flesh — crucifixion, resurrection — we need to look at the account in the Book of Genesis and then the commentary on the story in the Book of Hebrews.

The story begins,

> *"God tested Abraham. He said to him, 'Abraham!' 'Here I am,' he replied. Then God said, 'Take your son, your only son, Isaac, whom you love, and go to the region of Moriah. Sacrifice him there as a burnt offering on one of the mountains I will tell you about.' Early the next morning Abraham got up and saddled his donkey"* (GENESIS 22:1–3).

God tested Abraham. The word *test* is better translated "proved." When God tests, He is not trying to discover what is inside us. He knows what is inside us. He is *proving* what is inside us. He is bringing what is inside to the outside. Don't think of this as a "trick" on God's part. He is not trying to trip Abraham up; He is proving to Abraham what God knows is in him and He is using this crisis moment to free Abraham of his flesh. In the Book of Hebrews, we have an explanation of God's dealing with Abraham.

> *"By faith Abraham, when God tested him, offered Isaac as a sacrifice. He who had received the promises was about to sacrifice his one and only son, even though God had said to him, 'It is through Isaac that your offspring will be reckoned.' Abraham reasoned that God could raise the dead, and*

figuratively speaking, he did receive Isaac back from death"
(HEBREWS 11:17–19).

You remember the story. Just as Abraham was about to plunge the knife
into Isaac, the LORD stopped him. Yet the writer of Hebrews says, "Abraham
offered Isaac." He uses a verb tense that indicates a completed action. In
the Amplified Bible it is translated like this: "Abraham completed the
offering of Isaac." Didn't Abraham stop short of completing the offering?
Yet the Bible says that he offered Isaac, completing the sacrifice. When did
Abraham complete the offering of Isaac?

Go back to the account in Genesis. In the abbreviated version, God
called Abraham to offer Isaac as a sacrifice, and the next morning Abraham
got up and saddled his donkey for the trip. But between God's call and
Abraham's obedience lay a long, dark night of struggle. You and I are left
to imagine how intense that struggle must have been. We can guess at the
agony through which Abraham passed. Our hearts hear Abraham crying
out something like this: "If You would, let this cup pass from me!" And
before the morning broke, we hear him just as clearly say, "Nevertheless,
not my will, but Yours be done." It was in that dark night that Abraham
completed the offering of Isaac. Here we realize that it was not Isaac's
crucifixion but Abraham's. It was there that God received what He was
asking for. How do I know that?

One of the layers of meaning in this account is that it is a picture of
the Crucifixion. Follow the timeline with me. Abraham got up, saddled
his donkey, and set out for the place God would show Him (Genesis
22:2). He traveled for *three days* (Genesis 22:4), then took Isaac to the
top of the mountain and prepared to sacrifice him on the altar. Instead
of killing Isaac, God stopped him and Abraham received Isaac back in a
resurrection: "And figuratively speaking, he did receive Isaac back from
death" (Hebrews 11:19). If Abraham traveled for three days and on the
third day received Isaac back in a type of resurrection, then when was the
crucifixion? The sacrifice was completed on the long, agonizing night that
brought about Abraham's yielded obedience. Three days later, Abraham
received Isaac back in a resurrection.

God considered the sacrifice to be completed. God got what He was
after. What was God wanting from Abraham? What was the sacrifice?

Abraham was connected to Isaac in two ways: First, Isaac was the son
of his flesh. He was to Abraham "your son, your only son, Isaac, whom you

love" (Genesis 22:2). You can imagine how very strong that connection was. After having waited and yearned for this son until all rational hope was gone and his and Sarah's bodies were long past childbearing years, at last Isaac was born. As his son, in the days of Abraham, Isaac was his property. He had the right to do with him as he chose. You know that every choice Abraham made concerning Isaac was made out of an overflow of love.

Abraham was connected to Isaac in another way. Isaac was also the child of promise, born by the power of the Spirit (Galatians 4:28–29). It was through Isaac that all of the promise of God—that which had defined Abraham's entire adult life—was to be realized. "He who had received the promises was about to sacrifice his one and only son, *even though God had said* to him, 'It is through Isaac that your offspring will be reckoned'" (Hebrews 11:17–19, emphasis added). Abraham was connected to Isaac spiritually. Isaac was to Abraham both the child of his flesh and the child of the promise.

On the night that Abraham completed the offering, Abraham died to his flesh connection with Isaac. He let his father flesh die. He relinquished ownership. That was the night he laid Isaac on the altar. It was Abraham's crucifixion, not Isaac's.

In requiring Abraham to die to his flesh connection, God did not require Abraham to die to the spiritual promise. Abraham, I believe, was more alive than ever to the promise in Isaac. As he reached the place of the sacrifice, "he said to his servants, 'Stay here with the donkey while I and the boy go over there. *We will worship* and then *we will come back to you*'" (Genesis 22:5, emphasis added). The writer of Hebrews says, "Abraham reasoned that God could raise the dead, and figuratively speaking, he did receive Isaac back from death" (Hebrews 11:19). By the time he had become fully yielded to the voice of God, by the time he had dealt the death blow to his own flesh, he had reached a new level of faith in God. He was absolutely certain that, no matter what path the promise took, the promise of God would not fail.

Mary's Crucifixion

Imagine Mary as she stood at the foot of the Cross, watching the last drop of life drain from the body of her son. Surely she remembered the visit from the angel of the Lord as if it were only yesterday when he announced to her that she would give birth to the Promised One.

Mary, as she stood watching the Promise die, did not know about the resurrection. As she watched the Promise shed His blood on the altar, she didn't understand that by losing Him, she would be gaining Him for all eternity. By giving up her son, she received her Savior.

Circumcising Your Flesh

When Abraham's promise was about to be born, the last rite that God demanded of him was the covenant of circumcision. Before the promise could be born, Abraham's flesh had to be cut off. Let me say this a delicately as possible. The very part of Abram's body from which Isaac will receive life must be circumcised of flesh. Isaac must come from "the covenant in [Abram's] flesh" (Genesis 17:13). Jesus said, "Flesh gives birth to flesh, but the Spirit gives birth to spirit" (John 3:6).

When the nation of Israel responded to the promise of God in their flesh—when they refused to enter the Promised Land because they were fueled by fear—God declared that none of that generation would enter the land. Flesh cannot inherit the promise. Flesh cannot function in the realm of faith. When that generation of flesh had died, then the people could enter the land. Notice what had to happen as soon as they crossed over and set up camp in the land. Before they could occupy the land and subdue their enemies, God commanded Joshua to circumcise them. No one had been circumcised in the desert, while they wandered in the land of their flesh. But nothing could go forward in the Promised Land until all flesh had been circumcised.

> "Now this is why he did so: All those who came out of Egypt-all the men of military age-died in the desert on the way after leaving Egypt. All the people that came out had been circumcised, but all the people born in the desert during the journey from Egypt had not. The Israelites had moved about in the desert forty years until all the men who were of military age when they left Egypt had died, since they had not obeyed the LORD. For the LORD had sworn to them that they would not see the land that he had solemnly promised their fathers to give us, a land flowing with milk and honey. So he raised up their sons in their place, and these were the ones Joshua circumcised. They were still uncircumcised because they had

not been circumcised on the way. And after the whole nation had been circumcised, they remained where they were in camp until they were healed" (JOSHUA 5:4–8).

Crucifixion of our flesh is what releases the power of resurrection through our lives. Getting the flesh out of the way is what reveals the life of Christ in us. Cutting off flesh opens the way into the Promised Land of rest. Living in an altar'd state is the secret to power and victory.

REFLECT

Summarize in your own heart what God has spoken to you in these forty days.

Books by
Jennifer Kennedy Dean

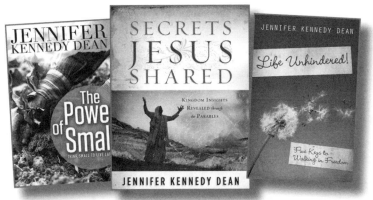

The Power of Small
*Think Small
to Live Large*
978-1-59669-313-5

Secrets Jesus Shared
*Kingdom Insights Revealed
Through the Parables*
978-1-59669-108-7

Life Unhindered!
Five Keys to Walking in Freedom
978-1-59669-286-2

Heart's Cry
Principles of Prayer
978-1-59669-095-0

Set Apart
*A 6-Week Study
of the Beatitudes*
978-1-59669-263-3

Live a Praying Life!
*Open Your Life to God's
Plan and Provision*
978-1-59669-299-2

Available in bookstores everywhere

For information about these books or any New Hope product,
visit www.newhopedigital.com.

New Hope® Publishers is a division of WMU®, an international organization that challenges Christian believers to understand and be radically involved in God's mission. For more information about WMU, go to www.wmu.com. More information about New Hope books may be found at www.newhopedigital.com. New Hope books may be purchased at your local bookstore.

Use the QR reader on your
smartphone to visit us online at
www.newhopedigital.com

If you've been blessed by this book, we would like to hear your story.
The publisher and author welcome your comments and
suggestions at: newhopereader@wmu.org.